The Floater's Guide
to MONTANA

The Floater's Guide
to MONTANA

Hank Fischer

Falcon Press Publishing Co., Inc.
Helena and Billings, Montana

FALCON PRESS

Library of Congress Number 86-81309

ISBN 0-934318-89-1

Distribution and Marketing: Falcon Press, P.O. Box 279, Billings, MT 59103
Editorial and Production: Falcon Press, P.O. Box 731, Helena, MT 59624
Editor: Bill Schneider
Cover Photo: Mike Sample
First Printing: August 1979
Second Printing: April 1981
Third Printing: May 1986

Contents

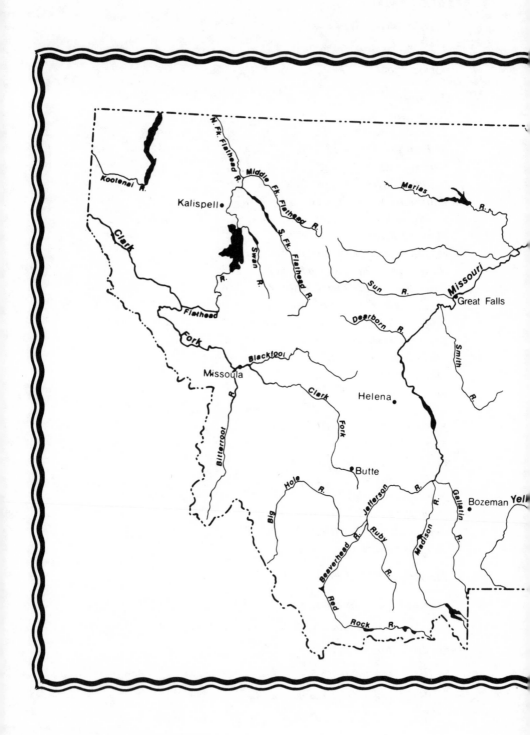

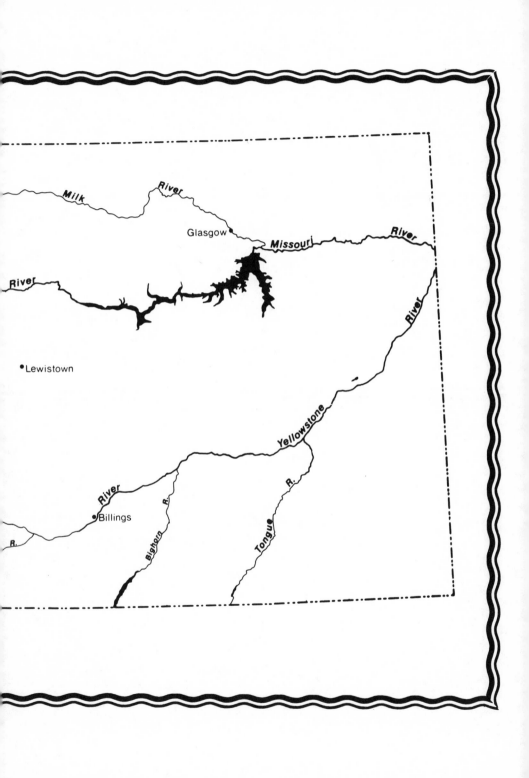

Introduction

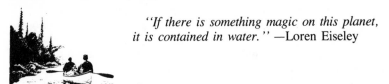

"If there is something magic on this planet, it is contained in water." —Loren Eiseley

Most people carry an "escape" dream, an idyllic plan for the time when life becomes too harried or complicated. For some, the dream takes them on a long wilderness trek. Others hope to sail off to sea. For many, the fantasy is simpler. Put a canoe or raft in the nearest river, lie back, let the sun warm the body, trail a hand in the water, and drift away.

It's a dream that started with the excursions of early river explorers like Lewis and Clark and John Wesley Powell. It's been kept alive by writers like Mark Twain, Ernest Hemingway, and Bernard DeVoto, and now it's being relived by modern river runners.

Montana's rivers have a special kind of historical significance, as the waterways played a key role in the Treasure State's early development. In early times the rivers carried only Indians and intrepid explorers. Later, they brought miners, cowboys, sod busters, soldiers, and shopkeepers. Indian bull boats and French pirogues were gradually replaced by flatboats and even steamships. It was only with the coming of the railroads in the late 1800s that Montana rivers faded in importance.

One reason the rivers were so important is that they are easily navigated. Despite the cold waters and rapid flow, most Montana rivers can be floated by people with only moderate river skills. Those who have seen Montana's towering mountains often find this hard to believe, as did Captain Lewis of the Lewis and Clark Expedition. He noted in his journal of 1805, "I can scarcely form an idea of a river running to great extent through such a rough mountainous country without having it's stream intersepted by some difficult and dangerous rappids or falls, we daily pass a great number of small rappids or riffles which descend one to or 3 feet in 150 yards but we are rarely incommoded with fixed or standing rocks and altho' strong rapid water are nevertheless quite practicable & by no means dangerous."

The vast majority of Montana's rivers lie in the mountainous western portion of the state, and flow down broad valleys between mountain ranges. In arid eastern Montana where only a few major rivers flow, the streams are generally broad and flat as they cut through open grassland and sagebrush country. While the sparkling western streams may be more spectacular, the eastern rivers have a quiet beauty and offer better opportunities for solitude.

On most Montana rivers, white-water sections occur primarily in narrow canyons and last only a few miles (check the special white-water section for a complete rundown). While some of the white water is extremely challenging, most individual runs can be covered in a day. Unlike some other western states, Montana has few rivers

1

suitable for extended white-water trips.

Montana rivers have a distinctly different appeal. They offer a deep sense of history and adventure still easily felt. In many instances, floaters can follow the river routes of early explorers, and if diligent enough, can seek out the same campsites that were used many decades ago. Some rivers have changed only slightly since early days, and floaters may travel for a week and see only a few bridges and farmhouses.

As the rivers wind through secluded canyons, heavily timbered bottomlands or isolated marshes, one can observe eagles, deer, bighorn sheep, osprey, bear, and waterfowl. More than anything else, wildlife sightings are the highlight of Montana float trips. Watching an osprey catch a fish, floating past a great blue heron rookery, or seeing a deer with newborn fawns are sights that remain etched on the memory. Quiet floaters often won't disturb wildlife as they drift by, allowing excellent opportunities for observation and photography.

Outstanding trout fishing lures many people to Montana rivers. Fisheries biologists report that some streams contain more than a ton of trout for each mile of stream; other rivers hold a trout two pounds or larger for every 10 feet of streambank, and a four-pounder or larger for every 20 feet. Montana has about 450 miles of blue ribbon trout water, and most of it can be floated.

Canoes and rafts not only allow a quiet approach, but they take fishermen to secluded portions of rivers not often visited on foot. Float fishermen often become addicted to this style of angling.

This book is written in hopes that everyone who experiences Montana's rivers will become addicted to them. Anyone who has floated a free river, relished its natural beauty, fished for its wild trout, or challenged its white water should resent its destruction. Hopefully, a day or more on some of Montana's sparkling streams will give floaters a personal stake in the rivers' future.

Caring for rivers

If floaters are careful, rivers can be floated again and again without showing any sign of use. Your attentiveness to caring for the river could preclude the need for permit systems that control the amount of use. Floaters on overnight trips should be especially mindful of their activities. Here are a few suggestions:

• Wash yourself and your dishes away from the campsite and at least 100 feet from the river. Use biodegradable, non-phosphate soaps or detergents. Bury your dishwater, food drainings, and wet garbage in your latrine.

• Bury human wastes at least 100 feet above the river's high-water mark. Campers should dig a latrine.

• Don't destroy vegetation at your campsite. Use only dead wood for firewood, and don't dig trenches or build shelters, bough beds or lean-tos.

• Don't build a new fire ring if an old one is available. Keep your fire small, and before leaving, scatter the rocks and leftover firewood. Throw the ashes in the river and reclaim the fire scar with topsoil. (When building a fire, set aside the sod and topsoil for reclaiming the fire pit.) Use a portable stove or build your fire in a fire pan (an old garbage can lid works fine) whenever possible; you won't blacken rocks and can dump your ashes in the river more easily.

• Erase all traces of your presence when you break camp. Remove all foil, glass, and unburned paper and plastic from the fire and pack it out. Remember cigarette butts and pull tabs are litter, too.

• Pick up and pack out garbage that less sensitive visitors have left along the shores or in the river.

How to use this guide

It isn't the intent of this book to provide a mile-by-mile guide to Montana's rivers. To the contrary, my purpose is to introduce floaters to Montana rivers and tell the minimum amount necessary for a safe, enjoyable trip. Knowing everything is like having someone tell you how a movie ends; discovery and exploration are an integral part of any river trip.

Additionally, this book only includes what I consider to be the major floating rivers of Montana. Many other rivers in the state have excellent floating potential, although usually only for short stretches or at certain times of the year. Some of these rivers can't sustain much floating pressure, so it's best for individuals to scout out specific floats on their own. Sections of the Bull, Clark's Fork of the Yellowstone, Clearwater, Boulder, Musselshell, Poplar, Judith, Teton, Yaak, Rock Creek, and Powder rivers can be floated. In addition, white-water enthusiasts (experienced) sometimes run small rivers and creeks during the runoff period.

I've chosen not to use the international scale of river difficulty (which rates rivers on a I-VI scale) in the main part of the text. (It is used in the special white-water section.) There are two reasons for this; first, most people aren't familiar with the system. Second, Montana rivers are too changeable—from month to month as well as year to year—to use this system in a meaningful way. Instead, I've simply rated the rivers on the skill required by the paddler.

This allows for certain variability. Certainly beginning rafters can negotiate some rivers beginning canoeists cannot, simply because of the inherent stability and buoyancy of good inflatable crafts. On the other hand, rafters might want to avoid some of the small, slow, winding streams where canoeists do fine.

Here's how I rate the different levels of paddling skill:

Beginner. Knows the basic strokes (for canoeists: front paddle, back paddle, draw stroke and pry stroke) and can handle his craft competently in smooth water. Knows how to bring the boat to shore safely in fast current, can negotiate sharp turns in fast current, can avoid log jams and other obstructions. Knows of hazards he might encounter and understands the difficulty of the stream he intends to float. *A beginner is not a person who is picking up a paddle for the first time.* Novices should get some practice on a lake or with an experienced floater before taking the first trip alone.

Intermediate. Knows basic strokes and uses them effectively. Can read water well and negotiate fairly difficult rapids with confidence (knows how to safely catch an eddy). Won't panic and knows what to do in the event of an upset. Knows how to coordinate strokes between bow and stern and can paddle at either end. Can come to shore quickly to inspect dangerous spots, and knows when to portage.

Expert. Has mastered all strokes and uses them instinctively. Confident of own ability even in very difficult situations. Skillful in heavy water or complex rapids. Knows when a rapid is unrunnable and has a deep respect for all safety precautions. Doesn't need to read guidebooks, but does anyway and tells friends to.

Remember, this guide only contains the minimum information needed for a safe trip. Thoroughly check out the stretch or river you plan to float before launching your craft. Rivers are living, dynamic systems that change constantly. A channel free of barriers one year may contain a dangerous logjam the next. Or, someone may have built a diversion dam (or strung up some barbed wire) which creates a hazard.

Carefully check water conditions before starting any trip. Montana Department of Fish, Wildlife and Parks and U.S. Forest Service offices are usually good places for information. Sporting goods stores can often provide information as well.

While the river adventurer won't face the perils of Odysseus—Sirens, Cyclops, or giant whirlpools—floaters should be aware of the many hazards that await them. These include diversion dams, fallen trees and logs, weirs, and fast water studded with rocks. Know in advance how to deal with each hazard, and know what to do in the event of an upset.

About the maps

The maps that accompany the text are meant to give the big picture; the scale is generally too small to adequately estimate mileage. Floaters can use them to select segments of rivers they wish to float and then find more detailed maps to identify landmarks and judge mile-by-mile progress. I've included a map appendix (page 135) listing detailed maps available for each river.

When using the maps in this guide, pay careful attention to the scale, as they vary considerably. Obviously, a map of an 80-mile river gives more detail than one of a 200-mile river.

I've tried to include all bridges and official public access points on the maps. Bridges obviously occur where roads cross rivers, but in a few places where space was sparse, they are marked with an "X." A triangle marks all official public access points— Forest Service, Bureau of Land Management, and Fish, Wildlife and Parks.

Some access points where roads run next to the river or where old roads and trails lead to the river haven't been included. Many of these "local" access points are privately owned, so ask permission before launching. Again, consult the map appendix for maps that show all roads and land ownership.

Floating and the law

Landmark changes have taken place in recent years regarding Montana's stream-access laws. These changes were initiated by lawsuits involving access disputes on the Beaverhead and Dearborn rivers. In 1984 the Montana Supreme Court ruled the public has a right to recreational use of the state's waters up to the high-water mark.

Then in 1985, the Montana Legislature passed a stream access law that even more narrowly defines the issue. The new law states that rivers and streams capable of recreational use may be so used by the public regardless of streambed ownership; the law also states that certain activities require landowner permission. The law only addressed river and streams, not lakes.

The law defines "recreational use" as floating, fishing, hunting, swimming, and other water-related pleasure activities. It defines the ordinary high-water mark as the line the water impresses on land by covering it for a sufficient time to cause different characteristics below the line, such as deprivation of the soil of substantially all its terrestrial vegetation and destruction of its value for agricultural vegetation.

The law divides the state's rivers and streams into two categories, Class I and Class II. Class I are those streams which are capable of recreational use and have been declared navigable or which are capable of certain kinds of commercial activity, including commercial outfitting. Class II rivers are all others. For the most part, all of the rivers discussed in this book are Class I streams, with the exception of the headwaters of a handful of rivers. The Montana Department of Fish, Wildlife and Parks has made a preliminary classification of the state's rivers that speaks to specific river segments (see Appendix II, page 132).

On both Class I and Class II streams, landowner permission is required for the follow-

4

Osprey, common along many Montana rivers. Harry Engels photo.

ing recreational activities, *even if these activities take place between the high-water marks:*

• overnight camping within sight of, or within 500 yards of, an occupied dwelling (whichever is less).

• big game hunting, although the Montana Fish and Game Commission has the authority to specifically authorize shotgun or bow and arrow hunting for big game between the ordinary high-water marks without landowner permission.

• making recreational use of stock ponds or private impoundments fed by intermittent streams.

• making recreational use of water diverted from a stream, such as an irrigation canal or drainage ditch.

• the placement or creation of a permanent duck blind, boat moorage, or any seasonal or other objects within sight of, or within 500 yards of (whichever is less), an occupied dwelling.

Finally, the stream-access law says that floaters using a stream may go above the ordinary high-water mark to portage around barriers, but must do so in the least intrusive manner possible, avoiding damage to the landowner's property and violating his rights. A "barrier" is defined by the law as an artificial obstruction (like a fence or a bridge) which totally or effectively obstructs the recreational use of the surface water. The new law *does not* address portage around *natural* barriers, and does not make such a portage either legal or illegal.

Recreationists should also be aware of new trespass legislation passed by the Montana Legislature in 1985. This law states that lands can be closed to the public either by verbal communication or by actual posting. Posting requirements can be fulfilled in two ways. First is the standard process of a sign on a post, structure or natural ob-

The South Fork of the Flathead, in the heart of the Bob Marshall Wilderness. Carol Fischer photo.

ject. The new way, instituted in 1985, consists of painting a post, structure or natural object with at least 50 square inches of fluorescent orange paint. In the case of a metal fencepost, the entire post must be painted. Such notice must be placed at each outer gate and all normal points of access, as well as on both sides of a stream where it crosses an outer property boundary line. Some say using paint as a posting requirement could cause blaze orange to become the unofficial state color.

In any event, be mindful of trespassing on private property, and when in doubt, ask permission. A special brochure is available from the Montana Department of Fish, Wildlife and Parks that provides some of the finer points on stream access.

Have a safe trip

Although few people like to talk about it, floating in Montana can be dangerous. Not only are many streams powerful and fast, but they are also cold, even in summer. Therefore, hypothermia can be as big a danger as drowning. With proper caution and planning, however, these hazards can be overcome.

Several persons die in Montana each year due to floating-related accidents, and most deaths occur when the water is high. Floaters must use good sense and know their abilities when floating rivers in May and June. Remember, runoff can last into July.

Beginners should be particularly wary about trips during the high-water period or in cold weather. Statistics show that the overwhelming number of floating accidents (and deaths) take place in May and June when rivers may be running at three to four times their normal flow.

The rivers

*"It was kind of solemn, drifting down the
big, still river, laying on our backs looking
up at the stars, and we didn't ever feel like
talking loud...."* —Mark Twain

Montana offers the variety of rivers one might expect for a 600-mile wide state
with high mountains in the west and high plains in the east and a great deal of wild
country everywhere. For the white-water enthusiast, there are frothy streams like
the Middle Fork of the Flathead and the Stillwater; for the fisherman, there are world-
famous trout streams like the Madison and Big Hole; for the adventurer, there are
historic streams like the Yellowstone and the Missouri.

Despite the rugged and beautiful terrain these rivers drain, most are easily navigated
by beginning to intermediate boaters.

Big rivers, small rivers, rivers through remote wilderness areas, rivers through
Montana's largest cities. Peaceful rivers, perilous rivers. Rivers clear as frozen ice,
rivers with stories to tell. Take the time to listen.

The Beaverhead River

The Beaverhead flows for only 43 air miles. But if the Corps of Engineers ever
decided to straighten it—and I'm certainly not recommending it—the Beaverhead would
probably stretch halfway across Montana.

Sinuous and serpentine, from the air it looks like a swimming snake. Expect to
travel at least three river miles for every air mile.

Not only does the Beaverhead meander a great deal, but it also supports a jungle
of vegetation along its banks. The combination of deeply undercut banks and thick
brush provides the habitat that makes the Beaverhead one of the superior trout streams
in the country. Biologists estimate that some sections of the river contain more than
400 two-to-four-pound trout per mile and another 100 over five pounds.

The Beaverhead is formed by the confluence of Red Rock River and Horse Prairie
Creek at the present site of Clark Canyon Dam, about 20 miles south of Dillon. The
upper section of the river flows through a highly scenic but arid canyon edged by
house-sized boulders and hills carpeted with sagebrush. By the time the river reaches
Dillon, the valley opens up, and the Pioneer and Ruby ranges provide a scenic
backdrop.

North of Dillon, floaters should look for Beaverhead Rock, a notable historic landmark which juts about 150 feet above the river. Located just upstream from the State
Highway 41 bridge, it's the place where Sacajawea first recognized her homeland
while guiding Lewis and Clark through the Rockies. Viewed from many angles in
the large valley—and particularly near Sheridan—the rock bears a marked resemblance

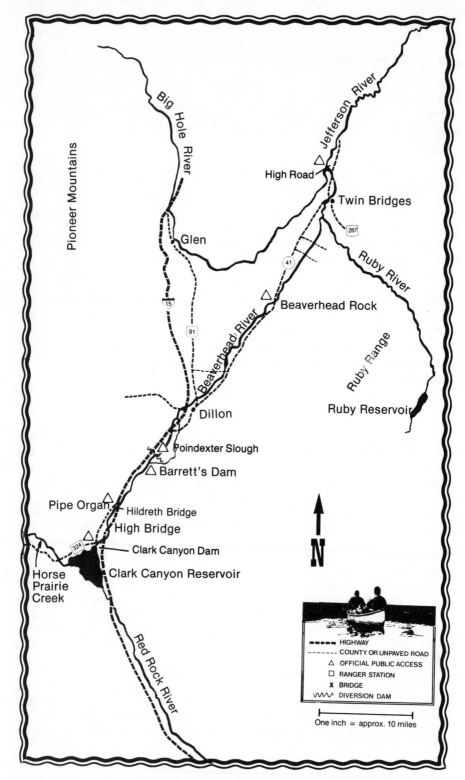

Beaverhead River

to a swimming beaver. Beaverhead Rock belongs to the Montana Department of Fish, Wildlife and Parks.

Don't expect to find crystal-clear water in the Beaverhead. Often it's downright murky, thanks to irrigation returns, overgrazing, and natural siltation. However the river's rich load of nutrients fosters the insects that make the trout fat and the trout fishermen happy.

Clark Canyon Dam causes some unusual water conditions for floaters. Early in the season (May, June and July), flows can be moderate as the reservoir is typically filling at this time. At a time of year when many rivers roar with spring runoff, the Beaverhead may have good floating conditions.

In the summer, water levels vary according to irrigation or flood control needs. In dry years, flows can be extremely low to the point where floating may be impossible. Flows may also get so low that they hurt fish populations; biologists cited 1977 as such a year. On the other hand, the 1984 flood also hurt the fishery.

During the fall when conditions are ideal on most Montana rivers, the Beaverhead may have high flows as water is released from the reservoir. This is particularly true in wet years. Before floating the Beaverhead, call one of the Dillon sporting goods stores to learn up-to-date water conditions.

When the water is high, floaters should beware of a low bridge (Hildreth bridge) about two miles below High Bridge. When the water is up, there may not be room for a boat to pass underneath the bridge. Other bridges are passable except in the most extraordinarily high-water flows.

While most of the Beaverhead has good access, the uppermost sections are very easily reached. Combined with good fishing, this makes the section between the dam and Barrett's diversion extremely popular. Many outfitters operate on this section of the river, and at times, the fishermen seem to outnumber the mosquitoes. It isn't a place of solitude.

Between Dillon and Twin Bridges, however, access is more limited and the river more isolated. There's more wildlife in this section, particularly white-tailed deer, great blue herons, beaver, and waterfowl. One can often see and hear sandhill cranes along the river, particularly at migration time. In the spring, watch isolated meadows for these ungainly birds performing their unique courtship ritual. Tundra swans are another Beaverhead migratory treat.

During the summer, whitetails often seek the coolness of the river to escape the heat and insects. One day, I counted almost a dozen deer half-immersed in the water. The Beaverhead also seems to support an inordinate number of owls. I once counted eight along one mile of river.

Floating the upper Beaverhead requires some skill, particularly above Pipe Organ Rock. Canoeists must be skilled at maneuvering around bends and down narrow channels, and rafters and other boaters must be good backpaddlers. The current can be quite swift in the upper 20 miles of the river, and the water can get very deep.

Intermediate paddlers won't have any trouble with the upper 20 miles of the river. Canoeists must remember, however, not to overload their crafts on winding rivers like the Beaverhead. Three people in the canoe or too much gear will cause problems even in an 18-foot canoe.

Floating is easier north of Dillon. The river still meanders repeatedly, but the current isn't as swift. When the water is low, beginners can handle this part of the Beaverhead all the way to Twin Bridges. Barbed wire across the stream as well as occasional diversion dams pose the biggest hazards. Again, watch for low bridges.

Float fishing is extremely popular on the Beaverhead, as much of the river doesn't lend itself to wading. According to biologists, the stream is very productive, sup-

Camping along the brushy Beaverhead. Hank Fischer photo.

porting a trout four pounds or better for every 20 feet of bank in some sections. But before you rush off to strap your boat on top of your car, please read a little farther. The Beaverhead offers some of the most frustrating and expensive fishing imaginable. The roots and bushes that extend into the water act like a safety screen for the fish and like a magnet for flies. Anyone with plans to fish the Beaverhead should have a full tackle box as well as a cheerful disposition.

The tackle box should contain a goodly assortment of Girdle Bugs, one of the most successful creations for catching canny Beaverhead trout. Developed by an often-thwarted Dillon angler particularly for the Beaverhead, this strange fly looks like it might be more at home on a lazy, southern bass pond. Consisting of a black or brown chenille body with trembling rubber legs, it reputedly was originally tied with the materials from a woman's girdle—hence the name. While some purists view this bundle of fuzz and rubber with disdain, it does resemble the crane fly, a long-legged insect that typically hatches on the Beaverhead in late summer.

Local nimrods tie the fly onto a 20-pound test leader and cast the monstrosity into the bushes with abandon. While there are enough fake flies on the bushes to confuse the real insects, it's rumored that the local fishermen do take a few trout.

The Big Hole River

When Oliver Wendell Holmes remarked, "A river is more than an amenity, it is a treasure," he could have been speaking about Montana's Big Hole River. Highly popular and nationally famous, its amber waters and pleasing scenery are dear to those familiar with this river.

The Big Hole received its name from early trappers, who called all valleys "holes." Since this was a particularly large valley, it earned the name Big Hole.

Before the trappers, the Shoshone Indians called the area Ground Squirrel Valley;

Lewis and Clark later named it Hot Springs Valley, after passing by the hot springs located a few miles east of the present site of Glen. Neither name stuck. In more modern times, travel brochures and Chamber of Commerce publications have dubbed it the Valley of 10,000 Haystacks. The Big Hole is one of the biggest hay-producing areas in the nation, and many ranchers still use the picturesque wooden "beaver slides" to stack hay.

There are few rivers in Montana as well-loved as the Big Hole. This picturesque river has a cult of followers—including fishermen, canoeists, and just plain river lovers—who would make Reverend Moon's disciples look downright apathetic.

George Grant, lifelong resident of Butte and an ardent conservationist, could well be the leader of this contingent. A dedicated river rat, Grant reportedly has spent more time on the Big Hole than any other person, alive or dead. While his comments might be biased, he once wrote, "In the nine great trout states of the western United States, it would be difficult to find a single stream that exceeds the overall quality of the Big Hole River. It must be classified as a big river, but it is certainly not as large or imper-sonal as the Yellowstone or Missouri, nor as barren-banked and monotonous as the famous Madison. The Big Hole rises at high altitude and flows clear and cold through wide valleys and narrow canyons, seldom presenting similar water or scenery throughout its entire 150 fascinating miles.

Intrepid floaters can start as high in the Big Hole drainage as Jackson. Here, the river is quite small and extremely sinuous, with many channels and obstacles. Barbed wire fences are common and sharp bends into overhanging branches are the rule. At high water, it's a challenge to stay out of the bushes; at low water, it's a challenge to stay off the bottom. The section from Jackson to Wisdom is isolated, interesting, and navigable by intermediates in canoe or kayak.

Adventurous types—but not beginners—may also want to try the North Fork of the Big Hole, starting at the Big Hole Battlefield. Here the river snakes through a maze of willow thickets and beaver ponds, replete with wildlife and accessible only by boat. It's only difficult when the water is high; there aren't any rapids, just an unrelenting current that always cuts into the bank and under the bushes. From year to year, there may be beaver dams to ford. This trip is particularly interesting in May and June when the birds are migrating through the valley and ducks, geese and sandhill cranes swarm to this excellent waterfowl habitat.

About 10 miles north of Wisdom, the river changes from a braided, winding stream, to a flat, broad river. From this point to the town of Wise River, the Big Hole is not particularly swift and presents few obstacles. This scenic section flows through high-altitude meadows alive with colorful wildflowers in the early summer. The protruding peaks of the Anaconda-Pintler Wilderness complete the scene. Once the water is low, it's a good float for beginners—easy access and few hazards.

The upper river provides excellent fishing, particularly early in the season. While it occasionally gets slightly discolored, it rarely gets muddy. Here, the river contains not only brook and rainbow trout, but also grayling. The upper Big Hole is virtually the only large river in the lower 48 where grayling can be caught with regularity. These beautiful fish, with their large dorsal fin and delicate black spots, are truly the Cadillac of the trout family.

The river between Wisdom and Wise River experiences high water temperatures in the summer and fishing may tail off. Rafting and swimming, however, come into their own, making this an ideal spot for a family float.

One word of advice for Big Hole floaters. Although the river is parallelled by major highways for most of its length, I've often had trouble hitchhiking back to my car after

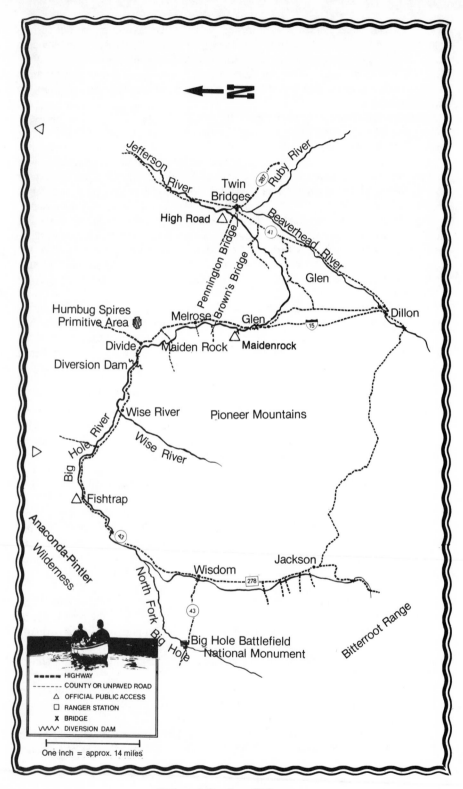

Big Hole River

Upper Big Hole River. Travel Promotion Unit photo.

a float. Much of the traffic is from out-of-state, and the flatlanders seem afraid of we backwoods Montana types. Carry a fishing rod or a canoe paddle to make the hitch-hike easier.

Below Wise River, the Big Hole occasionally gets fast and narrow as it continues to Divide. Beginners should get out before Wise River, as the canyon has some large waves and moderate rapids. Intermediates can handle this section, although open canoes may get swamped by high waves during runoff. Most of this section can be viewed from the highway. Watch carefully for the diversion dam at the Big Hole Pumping Station about half a mile above the highway bridge before Divide. It's very dangerous, and several people have drowned there.

The most heavily floated section of the river lies between Divide and Glen. Unof-ficial estimates run as high as 150 floaters per day during the peak period. Unques-tionably, the peak period occurs when the salmon fly hatch starts in mid-June. When these large insects hatch, the big trout—especially lunker browns—become unwary and can be taken readily on dry flies. This hatch is one of the state's most poorly kept secrets, however, and outfitters from all over the state (and country) haul their dudes in to get a piece of the action.

Because of the intensive fishing pressure, the Montana Department of Fish, Wildlife and Parks has designed special fishing regulations geared toward protecting trophy trout. While there has been talk of limiting the number of floaters during the salmon fly hatch, it appears the problem is somewhat self-regulating: when the crowds get too thick, those who want solitude go elsewhere, knowing in a few weeks fishing pressure will be very light.

Because of the large numbers of bank fishermen along the Big Hole, floaters should be especially courteous and considerate. Keep as far away from the fishermen as possible or go behind them if it's convenient.

The river flows through a canyon between Divide and Melrose which can be dif-ficult during high water. Intermediates in open canoes can make it, but don't count on doing much fishing. Most fishermen use rafts or river boats in this section. Between Melrose and Glen, the river is easier, although occasional diversions can cause problems. Beginners can handle this except when the water is up.

From Glen to the Big Hole's confluence with the Beaverhead, floating pressure is not as heavy, as access is more difficult. Here, the river generally meanders through thick cottonwood bottoms with only a few rapids. It does braid and wind a great deal, however, and has some troublesome logjams and fallen trees. It's a little too much for beginners. Fishing remains good, particularly for brown trout.

Biologists estimate that the lower section of the river hosts a wild brown-trout population of about 380 fish per mile, with an average size just under two pounds. There are more fish per mile upstream, but they aren't as large, on the average, as the trout below Glen.

While the trout may not always bite, the mosquitoes are quite dependable along the Big Hole. Be sure to take repellent and appropriate clothes.

Wildlife abounds amidst the diverse riverbottom habitat of the Big Hole. In the upper sections of the river, moose prowl the willow thickets. If you encounter one of these behemoths, be sure to yield right-of-way. Beaver and mink are common, and the Big Hole is one of the few rivers where I've seen a river otter. I saw a pair of them during one late September Big Hole float, and one was so annoyed he barked at us until we were out of sight. Given the price on otter pelts, I hope he changes his ways.

The upper section of the river hosts large concentrations of waterfowl during the migration periods. The best time to view them is in the spring when nearly all of the ducks are in their full breeding plumage.

The sharp-eyed floater may also spot bighorn sheep along the Big Hole, particularly in the canyon between Divide and Melrose. Large hawks and eagles patrol the skies over the river, and kingfishers make themselves known via their distinctive machine-

Montana grayling—the Big Hole River supports the only large-stream grayling population in the lower 48 states. Dept. of Fish, Wildlife and Parks photo.

gun call. Both white-tailed and mule deer can be seen near the river.

As popular and delightful as the Big Hole may be, it also has problems. The Reichle Dam, an age-old irrigation and flood control project, has been proposed numerous times, only to be swatted down by vigilant Montana citizens.

Dewatering of the river is currently the biggest problem, as farmers and ranchers need the water for irrigation. Increasing demands for water can only mean less will be left in the stream for fish and wildlife, as Montana has no state law that guarantees minimum flows. Depleted flows not only mean less water, but they also mean elevated temperatures and less dissolved oxygen in the water, which is deleterious to the aquatic life. Montana sorely needs adequate instream water reservations to protect these exceptional rivers.

The Bighorn River

Steeped in history and shrouded in controversy, the magnificent Bighorn River starts among the glaciers of the Wind River Range in western Wyoming. In recent years the Bighorn has gained the reputation of being one of the best rivers in the entire U.S. for large trout. With tributaries such as the Wind, Shoshone, and Little Bighorn rivers, this is a big river, nearly as large as the Yellowstone near Custer.

As the Bighorn flows into Montana, it carves a rugged and scenic canyon that extends for nearly 50 miles. This great chasm winds and twists through the mountains in a tortuous course, its limestone and sandstone cliffs exuding the same brilliant colors and hues as the Grand Canyon of the Yellowstone.

After the canyon, the Bighorn winds through arid benchlands and thick cottonwood groves. The river is an oasis in the middle of a parched land, a belt of green that attracts many species of wildlife, including deer, beaver, and songbirds. During migration, waterfowl flock to the Bighorn.

According to a 1932 newspaper account, the Bighorn once contained formidable rapids. The story read, "This river is one of the most dangerous in America to traverse. Many have lost their lives in attempts to go down the rapids, while a few others succeeded in accomplishing the feat."

The famous mountain man, Jim Bridger, claimed to have shot the Bighorn Canyon on a raft made of driftwood logs. Bridger, however, was known to stretch the truth. He also said the rivers in Yellowstone Park steamed because they flowed so fast they got the river bottom hot.

The Yellowtail Dam has transformed the treacherous Bighorn Canyon into a flat-water paddle. The 525-foot-high dam, completed in 1967, backs up 71 miles of river. While a canoe trip through the canyon is still extremely scenic and isolated, the area is used primarily by powerboats and water skiers.

Jim Bridger was only one of the dozens of mountain men who trudged up the Bighorn on their way to the outstanding fur-producing areas along the Wind and Green rivers. Although little indication remains today, the Bighorn River is crammed with Montana history.

From Captain Clark's journals, it's evident that he knew the approximate size and location of the Bighorn. The river got its name from the large population of bighorn sheep in the area. In 1807, an enterprising Spaniard named Manuel Lisa constructed the first trading post in Montana, near where the Bighorn and Yellowstone rivers join. In future years, this spot became the site of forts, a projected city, and an army headquarters. All are gone today.

Near Yellowtail Dam, the remains of Fort C.F. Smith can still be viewed. It was built in 1866 to protect travelers using the Bozeman Trail. The trail crossed the river

Bighorn River as it flows through the Crow Indian Reservation.
National Park Service photo.

about three miles below the present site of Yellowtail Dam.

Construction of Yellowtail changed the entire character of the Bighorn River in Montana, to the delight of many anglers but to the detriment of much wildlife habitat. The river once carried a heavy silt load to the Yellowstone. Now, the dam traps the dirt.

The combination of less sediment and regular flows means the river no longer braids or creates islands. In fact, about 1,500 acres of islands have disappeared since 1967, a 50 percent decrease. While this habitat loss is especially significant to beaver, muskrats, and geese, other native wildlife associated with the river has also suffered.

On the other hand the combination of less sediment and cold flows from the bottom of the reservoir has created an outstanding trout fishery. The river is not only rich in vegetation, but it squirms with aquatic life like freshwater shrimp, minnows, and caddis-fly larvae. The river flows through limestone country, and consequently the water is quite mineralized and rich in nutrients. Such a favorable climate makes for incredible growing conditions for trout. For instance, on the Bighorn a seven-inch rainbow trout can become a 14-inch trout in the space of a year, about three times the normal growth rate. A fingerling brown trout can grow to 16 inches in three years. Only the Beaverhead River can match the Bighorn for sheer fish productivity.

The Bighorn's reputation really rests on its abundance of large trout. The largest on record from the Bighorn is a 29-inch, 16-pound rainbow. The "average" fish is slightly more than 14 inches. The Bighorn has almost 3,000 fish per mile over 13 inches, almost twice as many as the Madison and nearly three times as many as the Beaverhead.

These Bighorn fish facts are well known across the country, and this river has been a common feature for outdoor magazines. Consequently, its popularity has zoomed to the point where it can be quite crowded during the peak periods of July, August,

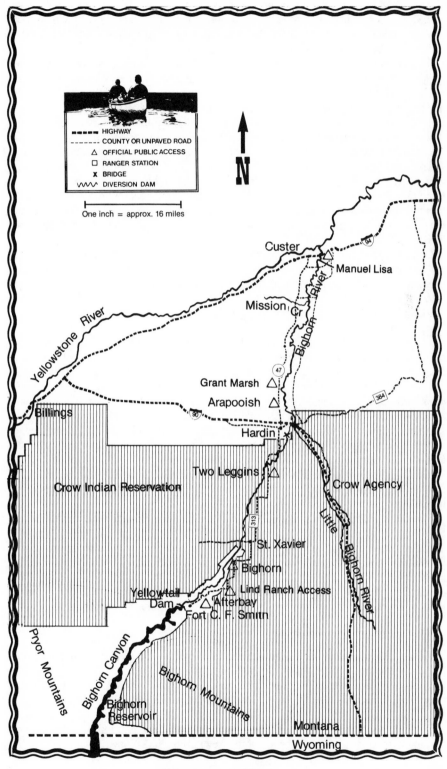

Bighorn River

and September. During this time the river may see 80-100 boats per day, with a great deal of guided traffic. Fortunately, the river can have good fishing almost any month of the year, so it is possible to avoid the crowds.

Fishermen can be handicapped during the peak of the summer by moss and algae buildups. Testimony to the productive nature of the river, the heavy salad buildup can make life miserable for spin fishermen. This same vegetation attracts all types of wildlife, and the birdlife along the river can be spectacular. Shorebirds pass through this drainage in large numbers, and the Bighorn sees heavy waterfowl use throughout the fall and winter. In fact, sometimes as many as 20,000 mallards winter on the river, and these ducks attract raptors like bald eagles and occasionally, peregrine falcons.

The upper 44 miles of the river flows through the Crow Indian Reservation, and recreational use of the river—particularly for fishing and hunting—has been a heated topic over the past two decades. In 1976, the Crow Tribe declared the river off-limits to non-tribal members. This initiated a legal debate that was ended by a 1978 Supreme Court decision that ruled the river bed belonged to the State of Montana, not the Crow Tribe.

Consequently, the river was reopened to fishing in 1981. Tribal members had hard feelings about this, and there were some confrontations; in more recent times, these problems have abated. Nevertheless, people using the portion of the river that flows through the reservation should be extremely mindful of staying within the high-water marks while fishing. Those hunting big game along the river must have landowner permission.

Access to the Bighorn is somewhat limited. Most floating takes place immediately below the dam, between the Afterbay and Bighorn access sites; this is about a 12-mile float. Below Bighorn, it's a 21-mile float to the next access, Two Leggins. This stretch can be floated in a day if you get an early start and don't stop much. The next access after Two Leggins is Arapooish, about seven miles downstream, just north of Hardin.

Below Hardin, the fishery is essentially warm water, with good fishing for sauger, shovelnose sturgeon, northern pike, and channel catfish. This section also has good waterfowl concentrations, and receives significant hunting pressure in the fall. The Crow Reservation stops at Hardin.

Floating pressure below Hardin is very light. Access can be difficult, however, as most of the river flows through private land. County bridges provide some access, but ask permission if they are posted.

Floaters use all kinds of crafts on the Bighorn, including motorboats and jet boats. Be prepared for some noise. With some caution, beginners can handle the Bighorn. The channel does split occasionally, and snags in the river can cause problems for the unwary. Rafters should watch for approaching windfronts in late spring and early summer.

Watch for the low diversion dam on the downstream side of the old Two Leggins Bridge. Below Hardin, watch for the Kemph and Manning diversion dams.

The Bitterroot River

When Old Bill Williams, the famous mountain man, found a river that pleased him, he would exclaim, "Thar my stick floats!'

My own stick floats in the Bitterroot, an occasionally battered but still beautiful river. Even though the river is close to civilization, it's excellent for a day-long or week-long float trip.

The Bitterroot retains much of the original beauty which early trappers and explorers frequently recounted. Captain Lewis of the Lewis and Clark Expedition provided this concise description in September, 1805: "It is a handsome stream about 100 yards wide and affords a considerable quantity of very clear water, the banks are low, and it's bed entirely gravel." Lewis and Clark originally dubbed the Bitterroot River "Clark's River."

Fringe benefits of floating. Dale Burke photo.

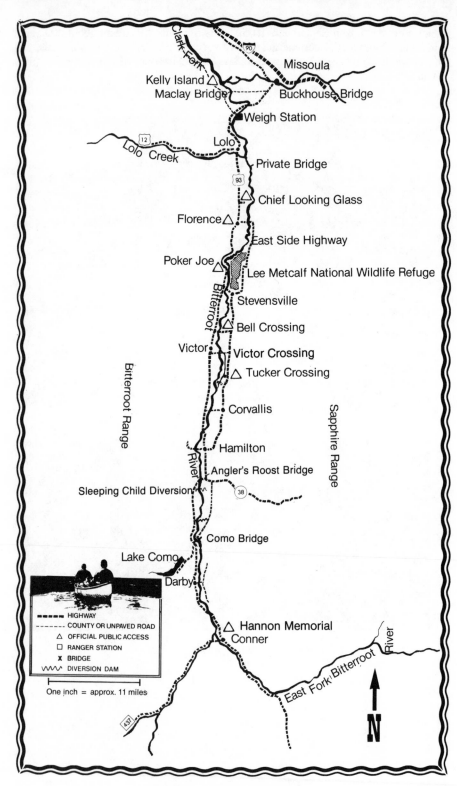

Kelly Island △
Maclay Bridge
Missoula
Buckhouse Bridge
Weigh Station
Lolo Creek
Lolo
Private Bridge
Chief Looking Glass △
Florence △
East Side Highway
Poker Joe △
Lee Metcalf National Wildlife Refuge
Bitterroot
Stevensville
Bell Crossing △
Victor
Victor Crossing
Tucker Crossing △
Corvallis
Bitterroot Range
Sapphire Range
Hamilton
Angler's Roost Bridge
Sleeping Child Diversion
River
Como Bridge
Lake Como
Darby
Hannon Memorial △
Conner
East Fork Bitterroot
River

HIGHWAY
COUNTY OR UNPAVED ROAD
△ OFFICIAL PUBLIC ACCESS
□ RANGER STATION
X BRIDGE
∿∿ DIVERSION DAM

One inch = approx. 11 miles

N

Bitterroot River

The proximity of the mountains makes the Bitterroot trips eminently scenic. The saw-toothed Bitterroot Range flanks the river on the west, while the more rolling and open Sapphire Range highlights the eastern horizon. The grass-covered Sapphires often light up spectacularly as the sun slides below the Bitterroots.

My favorite time for a Bitterroot float is in the fall when the river comes alive with color and fish are feeding in preparation for winter. Water conditions are usually excellent, as irrigation slacks off after the first few hard frosts. I usually try and arrange a three-day, 30-mile trip for this time of year. Fishing—particularly with dry flies— seems to reach its peak about the same time the colors of the leaves reach their most brilliant moments.

Those interested in extended trips may want to float the entire 80-mile length of the river. It only takes five or six days, and the occasional access points and isolated islands make excellent campsites. Be sure to check maps to avoid private land. If camping within the river's high-water marks, be sure to pay attention to stream access regulations.

Although the Bitterroot retains its clear and impressive vistas, civilization has placed a heavy hand on some parts of the river. Extensive riprapping, using both crushed rock and car bodies, has created eyesores. Fortunately, using car bodies for riprap is now illegal; there is even a law that mandates the removal of junked cars from rivers. The impact of that law hasn't yet reached the section of the Bitterroot between Stevensville and Florence, where the banks are so heavily riprapped with auto bodies, it's very popular with antique-car afficionados and used-parts dealers. Local fishermen tell stories, however, of a huge brown trout that lives in the trunk of a '54 Buick.

Irrigation also places heavy demands on the Bitterroot's finite water supply, to the detriment of the fish and wildlife which can only survive if adequate flows remain in the river. In dry years, much of the Bitterroot gets seriously dewatered, and floating isn't possible. The problem is generally most acute in the vicinity of Victor, where the river branches into several small channels. Annual purchase of water from Painted Rocks Reservoir by the state has helped solve this problem while keeping ranchers happy.

Despite the problems, many sections of the Bitterroot retain good wildlife populations. Deer, mink, and muskrat are common, as are the dippers and sandpipers which scurry along the shores. Canada geese nest in the secluded areas and on islands, and beaver sign can be observed along most of the river. Of special interest are the great blue heron rookeries and osprey nests found in the areas where the river winds away from civilization. Near Stevensville, the river skirts the Lee Metcalf National Wildlife Refuge.

The Bitterroot is a good river for seeing the unusual. Once I saw a yellow-bellied marmot sunning itself in a tree. Another time, I was surprised to watch a young bull moose wade across the river. Local residents say that elk may even appear in the river-bottom following a hard winter.

The Bitterroot can be floated for its entire distance, and even its two forks can be navigated by those proficient enough to maneuver around logjams and through fast water. While the Bitterroot is an extremely popular float stream, the use is well-dispersed; no single stretch seems to suffer from overuse. While the access is adequate, it's limited enough that the river doesn't get overrun the way the Blackfoot sometimes does. On the Bitterroot, more access points could mean crowded floating.

Few floaters start any higher than the U.S. 93 bridge between Connor and Darby. (Floaters should have at least intermediate skills to start on East Fork or West Fork of the Bitterroot.) The upper section of the river, though it does have some subdivision problems, generally has less development than below Hamilton. There's a catch-

Winter fishing on the Bitterroot. Carol Fischer photo.

and-release fishing section between Darby and Como Bridge that has caused rather heavy summertime float-fishing pressure from outfitters.

Upstream from Hamilton, however, lie more sharp bends, logjams, and fast water than in the lower portions. Except when the water is very low, it takes an intermediate canoeist. Rafters shouldn't have any problems. Watch carefully, however, for the diversion dams between Darby and Hamilton. One located a few miles below the Como Bridge has only a small drop which can be negotiated by experienced boaters. Watch out for the Sleeping Child Diversion (about five miles south of Hamilton) as it drops several feet and must be portaged.

Downstream from Hamilton, the river gets progressively easier to handle. Between Corvallis and Stevensville, the river channels a great deal, creating fast turns and hazards that can cause problems for beginners. The channels change remarkably from year to year, with logjams sometimes completely blocking the main flow of the river. In years when the main channel goes to the east, watch carefully for the diversion dam between Corvallis and Victor near Tucker Crossing; it's a mandatory portage. This diversion can be avoided by taking the left channel a couple of miles upstream.

From about Stevensville downstream, beginners can handle the Bitterroot, although there are still snags and sharp turns. Floaters have a bad habit of underrating the Bitterroot, particularly during high water. Its large number of downed trees, logjams, and small channels make it very hazardous when the river is swollen with runoff. Extensive clearcuts in the upper watershed are one of the factors that cause a fast spring runoff.

Despite its often placid appearance, the Bitterroot can be sneaky. I've heard more lost-boat or river-disaster stories about the Bitterroot than any Missoula-area river. One friend (who has swamped twice on the Bitterroot, once with his elderly parents) claims the river contains phantom shifting sandbars, not visible to the human eye. Don't be so busy sunbathing or fishing that you miss them.

Fish in the Bitterroot can be very tempermental. Some days only rainbows will bite. On other days, only browns. On some days, they conspire and neither will strike. Then again, there are those few days when it isn't safe to drag your fingers in the water. Generally, only the section of the Bitterroot below Florence bridge is open to fishing all year, so be sure to check the regulations before you leave home.

While some people feel it's a bit late to preserve the natural values of the Bitterroot, many areas remain secluded and undeveloped. The river's proximity to major population centers make it very valuable both as a recreational and an aesthetic resource. The entire river corridor needs an organized planning effort if its natural values are to be maintained for the public. So far the Bitterroot Chapter of Trout Unlimited has been championing the cause, but they can always use help. Give it a thought next time you float the Bitterroot.

The Blackfoot River

While most streams run swiftly in the upper reaches and then slow down in the lower parts, the Blackfoot River does just the opposite.

A brushy meadow stream in its upper reaches near Lincoln, the Blackfoot picks up steam and offers some challenging white water before its juncture with the Clark Fork River near Bonner. Its churning water and splendid scenery attract crowds of recreationists from Missoula and the surrounding area, making it one of the more heavily used rivers in the state. Floaters use it much more than the Bitterroot or Clark Fork.

The Indians knew the Blackfoot as Cokalihishkit, meaning "river of the road to the buffalo." Tribes followed the river for its entire 100-mile length, crossing the Continental Divide at the place we know as Rogers Pass, and then traveled out to the plains that surround present-day Great Falls in search of bison. Fur trappers willing to risk encounters with the Blackfeet Indians also worked the river in the early days, as did timber companies which used to float logs down the river to the mill at Bonner.

Floating on the Blackfoot can start as high in the drainage as a few miles east of Lincoln, where the Landers Fork meets the main river. Since the river is quite small here, floaters may be stymied by logjams and downed trees, which can completely block some channels of the river. The upper river braids a good deal, and when water levels are down, floating may be impossible. With each tributary, of course, floating gets easier. Below the point where the North Fork enters, about 20 miles west of Lincoln, floating is usually possible all year.

Despite the difficulties, the section of river between Lincoln and the Scotty Brown Bridge offers some outstanding scenery and solitude as it meanders through undeveloped riverbottoms, occasional farmland, and secluded canyons. It's definitely the least-floated section of the Blackfoot; I've only seen another canoeist once in five trips.

Because of its undeveloped nature, the upper river supports a variety of wildlife. Once after rounding a sharp bend, I was treated to a close-up view of a mature bald eagle wading a riffle, searching for food. White-tailed deer, waterfowl, and beaver are also common.

Between where the North Fork of the Blackfoot enters and the Scotty Brown Bridge is a five-mile stretch known as Box Canyon. Steep cliffs rise from both sides of the river and the surrounding hillsides are blanketed with thick timber. Cliff swallows construct their mud nests in this section, and a variety of raptors reside here. While the river is quite rocky, with some ledges and dropdowns, the canyon has only one moderately difficult rapid.

Fishing can be good in the upper river, which has an abundance of insect life. Insect carapaces on the cliff walls tell of a significant salmon-fly hatch. It reportedly occurs rather unpredictably in the early summer. The upper river is basically a brown-trout fishery, with some rainbows and occasional Dolly Varden. Hopper imitations work quite well in the fall.

Although much of the upper river is fairly slow and flat, the numerous logjams,

23

occasional sharp turns, and narrow channels will pose problems for beginners. Canoes do best—they're easier to portage over logjams—but rafts are a possibility. Beginners can handle this section in the summertime, but should stay away during high water or cold weather. At the lower end of Box Canyon, about a half-mile above Scotty Brown Bridge, lies a sneaky rapid that can swamp the inexperienced or the unprepared. In fact, I once saw a brand new 18-foot Grumman canoe wrapped around the main rock in the rapid. Those who aren't trying to win white-water merit badges can easily walk around the rapid. Watch for a diversion dam about a quarter-mile farther downstream.

Two warnings for the upper river. Don't let the U.S. 200 sign directing you to Scotty Brown Bridge cause confusion. The bridge is less than a mile down the road. River Junction, a Department of Fish, Wildlife, and Parks access point and campground at the juncture of the north fork of the main river, is about 10 miles down the road.

Secondly, below the Highway 271 cutoff, the river stays well away from U.S. 200. Several county roads cross the river, but they're pretty lonely and hitchhiking back to your car can be difficult. Take along a friend who's a good runner for this trip.

The North Fork of the Blackfoot has limited floating potential for those willing to drag their crafts around logjams and blocked channels. It's strictly an early summer float in dry years. When the water is high, it's very challenging even for intermediates, especially above the Highway 200 bridge where there are some very difficult rapids.

The white-water section of the Blackfoot begins near the County Line fishing access site about four miles below Scotty Brown Bridge (see white-water section). At the risk of taking on water, expert canoeists occasionally try this section, as do intermediate rafters and kayakers. Large rocks stud the river here, creating turbulent currents. The rapids between Bear Creek Flat and the Clearwater Bridge are quite challenging.

Access to the lower Blackfoot (below Scotty Brown) is quite good, thanks mainly to cooperative private landowners and Champion International, Inc. Along with state and local agencies, they have formed a cooperative river management zone which protects the river and makes it accessible to the public. Along this 30-mile corridor (from Scotty Brown to Johnsrud Park), various sites have been designated for boat launching, day use, overnight camping, and other uses. A pamphlet which details these areas, as well as providing an excellent floating map, is available from the Department of Fish, Wildlife and Parks. Watch for signs and be sure to follow regulations, as it's only through the good will of the various landowners and corporations that this outstanding section of the river has been protected and made available to floaters. This cooperative management approach on the Blackfoot is being used as a national example of an innovative way rivers can be protected.

The section from the Roundup Bar all the way to Bonner is undoubtedly the most heavily used portion of the river. White water continues for a couple of miles below the Roundup Bar Bridge before the river flattens out. This is a good section for intermediate canoeists. From Ninemile Prairie to the Whitaker Bridge, floating is easy, and beginners should have no problems. Unique forms of wildlife make this a popular section. One area is known as "Bosom Beach," because of its summertime concentrations of unclad bathers. Red Rock, site of the once notorious Blackfoot Boogie, also lies in this section, giving it unique historical significance.

Beginners should pull out at the Whitaker Bridge, as the difficult Thibideau rapids lie not far below. If you try the rapids, stay to the right side of the river if you want to stay dry.

Next comes Johnsrud Park, probably the most common starting point for a Blackfoot float. The standard trip starts at the landing above McNamara Bridge and ends up at the weigh station near Bonner about four or five hours later. Once the water is low,

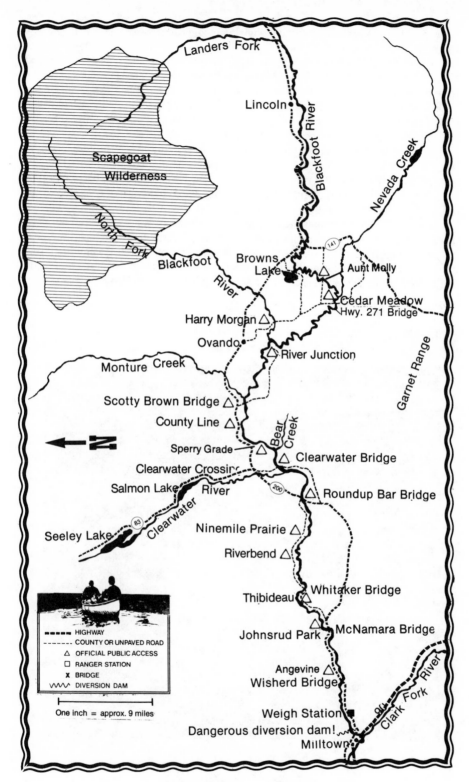

Landers Fork

Lincoln

Blackfoot River

Nevada Creek

Scapegoat
Wilderness

North Fork

Blackfoot River

Browns Lake

141

Aunt Molly

Cedar Meadow
Hwy. 271 Bridge

Harry Morgan

Ovando

River Junction

Garnet Range

Monture Creek

Scotty Brown Bridge

County Line

Bear Creek

Sperry Grade

Clearwater Bridge

Clearwater Crossing

Salmon Lake

Clearwater River

200

Roundup Bar Bridge

Seeley Lake

83

Clearwater

Ninemile Prairie

Riverbend

Whitaker Bridge

Thibideau

Johnsrud Park

McNamara Bridge

Angevine
Wisherd Bridge

Clark Fork River

Weigh Station

90

Dangerous diversion dam!

Milltown

- - - - HIGHWAY
- - - - COUNTY OR UNPAVED ROAD
△ OFFICIAL PUBLIC ACCESS
□ RANGER STATION
X BRIDGE
WWW DIVERSION DAM

One inch = approx. 9 miles

Blackfoot River

it's generally not a hazardous trip, although beginning canoeists should watch carefully for rocks and snags.

Floaters should beware of the dangerous diversion dam opposite the U.S. Plywood Mill at Bonner. Several people have drowned after floating over this dam. Signs upstream from this hazard provide warning, but it's best to take out at the weigh station at Bonner.

On a typical hot, summer weekend, the river between Johnsrud Park and the weigh station can be packed with rafts, canoes, kayaks, and inner tubes. Throw in fishermen and swimmers, and it can get rather congested.

Because of the burgeoning number of floaters (especially canoeists), anglers have come to refer to this midsummer phenomenon as "the aluminum hatch." It occurs very predictably on hot summer days. Floating beer bashes have also become a problem, and certain sections of the river have accumulated fine crops of beer cans. Take a bag along and clean up after our unthinking brethren.

Despite the cooperative management plan, the Blackfoot is not safe from development. The Corps of Engineers has been considering several dam sites, and even held public hearings on them in 1977. Although outraged citizens did everything but throw dead cats at the Corps during the public hearings, the proposals bear watching. The Corps has never been an agency to let adverse public opinion deter its plans.

The Clark Fork River

As recently as 1972, the Clark Fork River ran red with pollution, and even the most daring river runners didn't risk their necks on the placid-but-acid upper river. Thanks

Blackfoot River. Cal Tassinari photo.

to the Anaconda Company, all forms of aquatic life were wiped out in parts of the upper river and nearly 100 miles of stream were affected.

But this sad situation has improved markedly. Responding to pressure from private individuals and state agencies, the Anaconda Company began to clean up its act. The results were astounding. Sections with an average of four trout per mile in 1972 increased to an average of 984 catchable (over six inches) trout per mile in 1978. Aquatic insects had returned, as had much of the river-dependent wildlife.

While the Clark Fork still has some significant water quality problems, it has become one of western Montana's popular floating streams. It begins its 200-mile trek across the state near Warm Springs and can be floated for its entire distance in Montana. The upper sections are brushy and winding, the lower sections broad and deep. Where it exits the state on its way to meet the Columbia River, the Clark Fork River carries more water than any river in Montana, with a flow nearly equal to the Missouri and Yellowstone rivers combined.

The Milltown Dam, a small power project about five miles east of Missoula, creates the artificial distinction between the upper and lower river. The dam is at the head of Hellgate Canyon, an area named by French trappers. In early times, this was an ideal spot for ambushes and horse-stealing. Since enemies didn't worry too much about funeral arrangements, the place became so cluttered with bones and skulls that the Frenchmen called it "The Gates of Hell." If the origin of this name depresses you, keep in mind that Paradise—the site where the Clark Fork joins the Flathead— is a mere 80 miles downstream.

Interstate 90 parallels the Clark Fork for most of its distance in Montana. Fortunately, it's usually far enough from the river that one has a sense of solitude. Even though the river lies next to an interstate highway, access isn't always easy. County-road bridges, along with a few Department of Fish, Wildlife and Parks sites, provide most of the access.

On the upper river, floating can start right below the settling ponds at Warm Springs. For the uppermost 15 miles of the river, between Warm Springs and Deer Lodge, the river is quite small with many bends. After midsummer, plan on scraping and carrying your craft across riffles. Canoes are best at negotiating the sharp turns and avoiding the overhanging brush in this section. For those so inclined, this is a good section to paddle alone.

Don't miss the outstanding scenery as the river meanders past the Flint Range; sunsets can be spectacular. Beginners can handle this section when the weather is favorable and the water is low.

From Deer Lodge to Garrison, the river broadens and gets shallow, occasionally getting too low for floating after midsummer. Like the section above Deer Lodge, this part of the river receives little floating pressure. The Indians knew this part and the rest of the upper Clark Fork as the Arrowstone River because of a semi-transparent stone found near the river that was used to make arrowheads.

From Garrison to Drummond, water quality improves substantially, thanks to the addition of the Little Blackfoot River. This section of the river gradually winds away from civilization as it flows through thick cottonwood bottoms alive with whitetail and beaver. Although this section has a fair brown-trout fishery, dense algae growth often makes fishing difficult. In August the algae makes this section of the Clark Fork an unofficial dry-fly-fishing-only area. Anglers occasionally take cutthroat trout in this section, a species normally associated with high-water quality. In the fall and winter, the river is heavily used by ducks and geese.

The repeated bends, occasional diversion dams and barbed wire fences make the

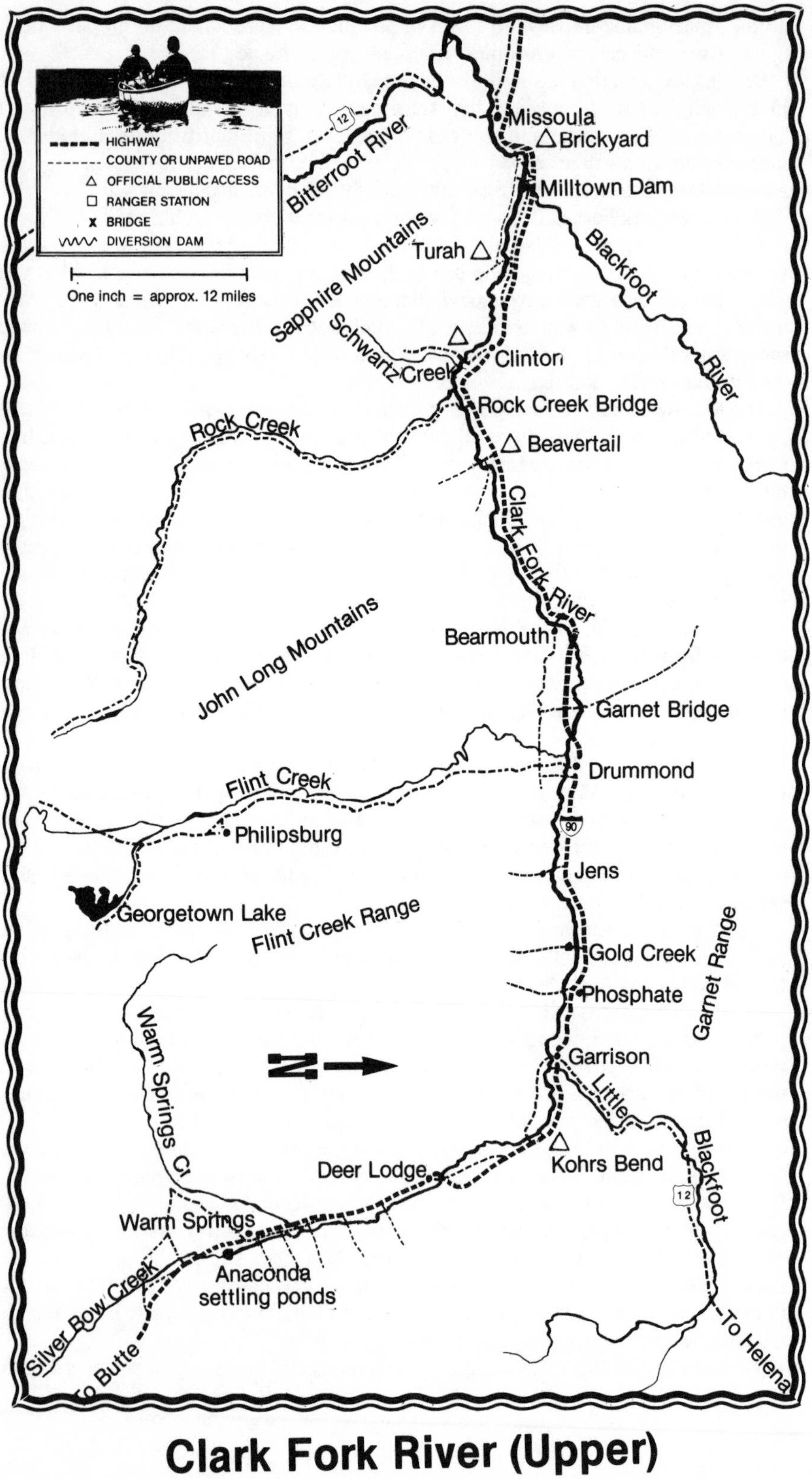

HIGHWAY
COUNTY OR UNPAVED ROAD
OFFICIAL PUBLIC ACCESS
RANGER STATION
BRIDGE
DIVERSION DAM
One inch = approx. 12 miles
12
Bitterroot River
Missoula
Brickyard
Milltown Dam
Blackfoot River
Sapphire Mountains
Turah
Schwartz Creek
Clinton
Rock Creek Bridge
Rock Creek
Beavertail
Clark Fork River
Bearmouth
John Long Mountains
Garnet Bridge
Drummond
Flint Creek
Philipsburg
90
Jens
Georgetown Lake
Flint Creek Range
Gold Creek
Phosphate
Garnet Range
Warm Springs Cr.
N
Garrison
Little
Blackfoot
Kohrs Bend
Deer Lodge
12
Warm Springs
Anaconda settling ponds
Silver Bow Creek
To Butte
To Helena

Clark Fork River (Upper)

Garrison-to-Drummond stretch a little too difficult for beginners except when the water is low. Much of this section flows through private land where landowners are very sensitive about trespassing, so stay within the high-water marks.

The section of the upper Clark Fork from Drummond to Milltown Dam is by far the most heavily used portion of the upper Clark Fork. Not only is it close to Missoula, but water quality is substantially improved when Rock Creek flows in. Most floats take place between Rock Creek and Schwartz Creek or between Schwartz Creek and Milltown. The fishing can be good, but it's not a well-kept secret.

Numerous downed trees, logjams, and tricky channels make the Drummond-to-Milltown run challenging when the river is high, particularly between Rock Creek and Milltown. Beginners would be wise to avoid this section altogether.

Wildlife sightings enliven most upper Clark Fork trips. Deer and waterfowl are common, and songbirds flourish in the thick brush. Look carefully for owls and osprey as well as marmots. Raptors can often be spotted where the river runs next to cliffs. Should you ever get behind schedule and have to paddle after dark, don't be surprised if a beaver whacks his tail on the water next to your boat. It's one of their favorite tricks.

In recent years, more and more fishermen have started floating Rock Creek. Because of frequent logjams and occasional rocks, it takes a strong intermediate to float this swift and narrow stream safely. Rock Creek typically gets too low to float by mid-July. Some people have voiced concern about the social conflict between float-fishermen and those who are wading. My advice to anyone thinking about floating Rock Creek would be to avoid the weekends when peak numbers of people are on the river.

Despite the good efforts of the Anaconda Company, water-quality problems and cloudy water associated with them are still the bane of the Clark Fork and provide the biggest disappointment for floaters. The source of the murk is not clear.

Biologists from the Department of Fish, Wildlife and Parks believe the cloudy water is caused by algae. At least two types of algae proliferate in the Clark Fork. One, a bright green algae, grows in strands off the river bottom and makes fishermen swear.

The algae believed to cause the murk, however, is a brown algae suspended in the water. Large amounts of nutrients in the water cause the atypical algae growth. The nutrient source could well be from poor agricultural practices, sewage, Anaconda Company, natural sources (there are large phosphate deposits nearby), or combinations of these factors. Studies are under way to investigate the problems.

In recent years, biologists have become more and more convinced that many of the most serious Clark Fork pollution problems can be traced to the headwaters where the river still cuts through old mine tailings. Federal funds have recently become available to try and remedy this problem.

The Clark Fork changes complexion and becomes a large, broad river after joining the Blackfoot and Bitterroot rivers near Missoula. The lower river flows mainly through cottonwood bottoms, though in some areas steep, pine-covered hillsides come down to the river's edge.

Although access to the lower Clark Fork is generally adequate, most floating takes place near Missoula. The section from the Milltown Dam to Missoula is quite popular and is the site of an annual canoe and raft race. While it really isn't very dangerous, one scuba diver reports this section of the water contains the remains of more than 20 canoes. Watch for occasional downed trees.

The lower Clark Fork probably offers the easiest floating close to Missoula, but beginners should stay away until after runoff. Man-made hazards such as diversions dams and weirs pose the biggest threat.

Those floating through Missoula should watch for a diversion just upstream from the Eastgate Shopping Center. Then, as you leave town, take the south channel. The northern channel has a diversion dam just above the confluence of the Bitterroot and Clark Fork that must be portaged.

Another close-to-town float that's very popular with Missoulians starts on the Bitterroot River at Maclay Bridge and ends six miles downstream at Harper Bridge on the Clark Fork. It's suitable for beginners and has good rainbow-trout fishing. Experienced floaters may want to try it in the winter, when the goldeneyes, mergansers, Canada geese, and eagles concentrate along the river; I once saw five mature bald eagles along this stretch on a bright winter day.

Below Harper Bridge, the Clark Fork winds past the odiferous pulp mill near Frenchtown and continues placidly until it reaches Alberton. Although the paper plant's stench might discourage you, this part of the river is very isolated and can have good fishing. The pulp mill wants to obtain a permit to continuously dump waste water from the mill into the river, which has caused a continuing controversy. The cottonwood bottoms sustain beaver and deer, and black bears occasionally wander down from the mountains.

Now far below Alberton, the river enters the Alberton Gorge, also known as Cyr Canyon. This stretch of water contains many rapids and much heavy white water (see white-water section). Experts with large rafts or kayaks can make it, but inexperienced floaters with canoes or small rafts don't have a chance. Commercial outfitters take groups or individuals on trips through this spectacular canyon.

Safe floating starts again near Tarkio and continues to Thompson Falls with only minor rapids. Beginners should portage Cascade Rapids—200 yards of difficult water—between St. Regis and Paradise. The other tough spot occurs right after Plains. Beginners may want to use the shoreline.

Much of the lower Clark Fork still has undisturbed shoreline, with mountains rising up from each side of the river. Like the upper river, the lower Clark Fork does have some water-quality problems, probably related to agricultural pollution. It couldn't be too bad, however, as the river has a rainbow-trout fishery few streams can match. In the fall, copious mayfly hatches bring the trout to the surface where they feed with abandon. The cold nights and warm afternoons bring on some of the most consistently good fishing experienced all year.

Motorboats and airboats threaten to become a nuisance on the lower river and could require regulation. In 1982, a commercial jet-boat tour business was started on the lower Clark Fork, but it tanked in a year. However, dam proposals by the Corps of Engineers pose a more serious threat. The Corps has been studying the feasibility of dams in the Alberton Gorge area, and local citizens have been telling them they don't want any.

Funny thing about the Corps, for as much as they get the needle, they never seem to get the point.

In 1984, a new citizens' group called the Clark Fork Coalition was formed to deal with the assorted Clark Fork environmental threats. If you're concerned about the Clark Fork, why not join? The address is Box 759, Missoula, MT 59807.

The Dearborn River

During my first Dearborn River trip, I was captivated by the extreme clarity of this small stream. Even in the deep pools, I could almost always see the brightly colored rocks that dot the streambed. A few months later, while perusing *The Journals of Lewis and Clark*, I was surprised to learn that Captain Lewis had made the same observation during his brief exploration of the Dearborn on July 18, 1805.

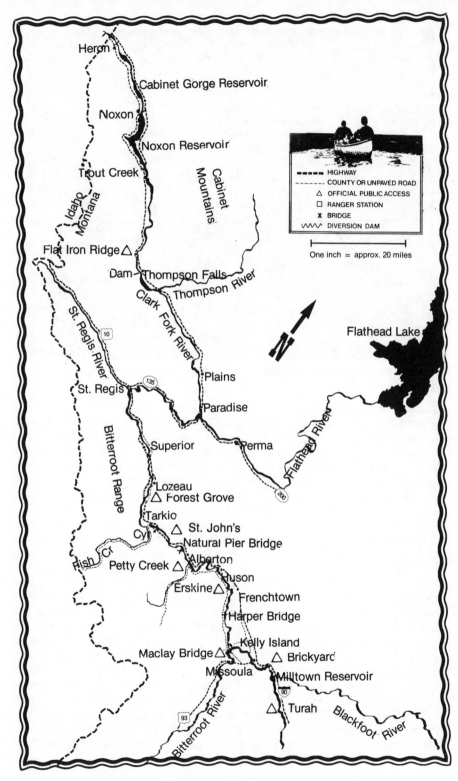

Clark Fork River (Lower)

River otter, disappearing symbol of the western waterways.
Dick Randall photo.

Captain Lewis wrote: "At the distance to 2 1/2 miles we passed the entrance of a considerable river on the Stard. side; about 80 yds. wide being nearly as wide as the Missouri at that place. it's current is rapid and water extreamly transparent; the bed is formed of small smooth stones of flat rounded or other figures. it's bottoms are narrow but possess as much timber as the Missouri. the country is mountainous and broken through which it passes. it appears as if it might be navigated but to what extent must be conjectural. this handsome bold and clear stream we named in honor of the Secretary of war calling it Dearborn's river.'

This picturesque stream gets its start high on Scapegoat Mountain, carving a deep and beautiful path as it winds its way through the former hunting grounds of the Blackfeet Indians. It's a relatively small, but high-quality stream with a floatable distance of about 45 miles.

The Dearborn can logically be divided into three one-day trips (more if you're fishing or taking pictures) with good access to each. Floating can begin as high as the Dearborn Canyon Road bridge, which is about four river miles above the Highway 434 bridge. The Dearborn Canyon Road bridge offers better access as the Highway 434 bridge has rather steep banks. From the Dearborn Canyon Road bridge to the Highway 200 bridge it's about 16 river miles. Here the river is very small and shallow with a gravel bottom; it's a very scenic section of river, but it's primarily an early-season trip, as it typically gets low by early July. Beware of a waterfall about 10 miles downstream from the Dearborn Canyon Road put-in. It's a mandatory portage. Watch out for occasional fences as well—some are not easily seen. Because it's a rather narrow canyon with many rocks, you should be a strong intermediate to try this one.

The middle section, from the Highway 200 bridge to the Highway 287 bridge, flows

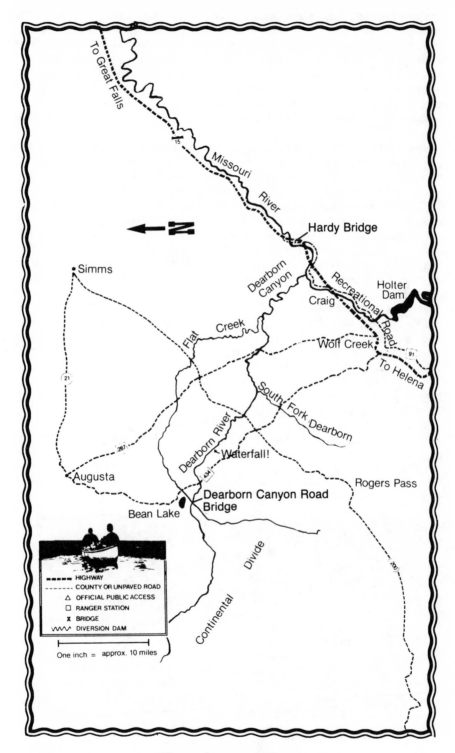

Dearborn River

for about 10 miles. This section generally runs through rolling farmlands with occasional bluffs. This section isn't nearly as difficult, but again, watch out for fences.

The most popular and scenic Dearborn float is from the U.S. 287 bridge to the Missouri River. Although the distance is less than 12 air miles, the river twists and turns through a narrow canyon, making the trip about 19 river miles long. With time out for photography and fishing, it can take two days. Most floaters will want to stay longer, as the river courses through a spectacular gorge, replete with sheer walls and unusual rock formations. The usual take-out is at one of the access sites on the Missouri River.

Beware, however, that the land within the canyon is almost completely private and there are very few good campsites within the high-water marks. Be extremely careful about trespassing on private property as this river has some very sensitive landowners.

Beaver, deer, and various birds abound along the Dearborn, and you might be fortunate enough to spot the disappearing symbol of our rivers, the otter. The Dearborn is one of the few rivers in Montana where I have seen otters.

Montana, unlike many other states, allows the taking of these fascinating creatures. They truly are an inoccuous animal; they don't eat sheep, grass, or people, and there's no surplus of them. They're endangered in many states, extinct in others. Although Lewis and Clark encountered them regularly in Montana, count yourself fortunate to ever see one.

Beginners should shy away from the Dearborn, as several swift spots interrupt the generally peaceful flow. While most of the tough sections only last for a short distance, some rapids last for 300 yards or more and require careful scouting—especially if you plan to run them in open canoes. Intermediates can handle these rapids except during the peak of runoff. Rafters may have problems, as the river alternates between shallow riffles and deep pools. Watch out for a small waterfall about halfway between the Highway 434 bridge and the Highway 200 bridge.

The floating season is typically quite short. The water is often high and dirty early in the year, and usually gets too low to float by mid-July.

The river offers excellent fly fishing for small rainbows and some cutthroats. A few large brown trout also reside in the deep pools. I was once reeling in a small rainbow (about eight inches) when a large brown dashed up from the bottom of a hole and grabbed the little trout. About a five-pounder, he gave me quite a struggle before letting go.

Tough spot in the canyon on the Dearborn River. Bob Buzzas photo.

The Dearborn offers some white-water canoeing. Hank Fischer photo.

For most of its floatable distance, the Dearborn offers a semi-wilderness float. Much of the canyon is relatively pristine. In some of the lower parts, however, subdivisions and others signs of human activities scar the river.

Obviously, some type of management is necessary for this spectacular river if it's going to keep its outstanding natural values. It would be a good candidate for wild-and-scenic-river designation, if it had a solid constituency. Even a cooperative management effort, like that on the Blackfoot River, would be a big step forward.

For a long time, it's been a river without a voice, but now the Medicine River Canoe Club in Great Falls has begun to work for the river.

The Flathead River

If Huck Finn had ever run away to Montana, he might have made the main branch of the Flathead his home.

It's a big, broad, peaceful river, the perfect spot to lay back in a raft or canoe and dream away a summer afternoon. Although its three magnificent forks often get more attention, the main Flathead offers scenic floats, suitable for beginners and close to civilization.

Floating on the main trunk of the Flathead begins near Blankenship Bridge where the North Fork meets the Middle Fork. Watch out for a rapid know as the Devil's Elbow just downstream from here. The South Fork enters a few miles downstream, just east of Columbia Falls; there are small rapids in this section.

The Hungry Horse Dam, located on the South Fork a few miles from the main Flathead, creates one of the main river's few hazards. Irregular water releases from the dam can cause unexpected water fluctuations of two to three feet, which speed

Canada geese on the Flathead River. Bob Ream photo.

up the current.

Otherwise, the river can be floated easily all the way to Flathead Lake. Below where the South Fork enters, it's easy enough for beginners and quite popular with local residents.

The river is particularly intriguing east of Kalispell, where it meanders through swampy lowlands. Here the river channels repeatedly, creating many islands. Old river channels have formed backwaters and sloughs loaded with waterfowl and beaver. Watch for ospreys diving for fish and great blue heron rookeries on the secluded islands.

The section of river immediately upstream from Flathead Lake receives heavy pressure from floaters, fishermen, motorboaters, and some water skiers. It gets particularly crowded when the kokanee salmon run upstream out of Flathead Lake in the late summer and fall. Large bull trout and cutthroat often lurk here as well.

Below Flathead Lake, easy floating resumes at the Buffalo Bridge about 10 miles downstream from Kerr Dam. Most floaters avoid the stretch immediately below Kerr Dam because of the formidable Buffalo Rapids—for good intermediates and experts only (see white-water section).

Below Buffalo Bridge, the Flathead flows tranquilly for 66 miles before joining the Clark Fork River near Paradise. This extremely scenic section of river rolls by steep cliffs and unusual badlands. Abundant wildflowers and occasional abandoned homesteads accentuate the broad vistas along this isolated and undisturbed portion. The clear, aquamarine waters add another dimension to a trip quite unlike any other in western Montana.

Bird watchers enjoy the great variety of avian life that darts and hops along the river; one group of floaters spotted over 70 species during a two-day trip. During migration, it's possible to see over a hundred species. Raptors are particularly prevalent, as the high cliffs provide excellent habitat. At least three breeding pairs of bald eagles are known to use the lower river. Many species of waterfowl nest along the river, and you may observe the special wooden nesting structures built for Canada geese. Motorboats

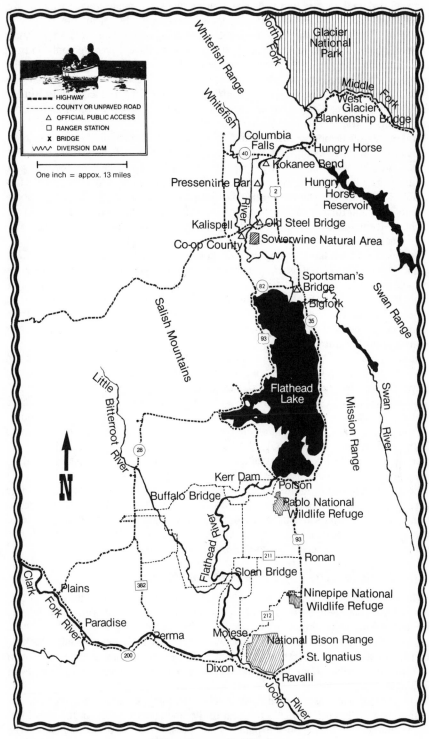

HIGHWAY
COUNTY OR UNPAVED ROAD
△ OFFICIAL PUBLIC ACCESS
☐ RANGER STATION
✗ BRIDGE
〰 DIVERSION DAM

One inch = appox. 13 miles

Glacier National Park

Whitefish Range

North Fork

Middle Fork

West Glacier

Blankenship Bridge

Whitefish

Whitefish

Columbia Falls

40

Hungry Horse

△ Kokanee Bend

2

Pressentine Bar △

Hungry Horse Reservoir

River

Kalispell

△ Old Steel Bridge

Co-op County

▨ Sowerwine Natural Area

Salish Mountains

82

Sportsman's Bridge △

Bigfork

35

93

Swan Range

Flathead Lake

Little Bitterroot River

28

Mission Range

Swan River

Kerr Dam

Polson

Buffalo Bridge

Pablo National Wildlife Refuge

Flathead River

93

211

Ronan

382

Sloan Bridge

Plains

Ninepipe National Wildlife Refuge

Clark

Paradise

Fork

River

Perma

212

Moiese

National Bison Range

St. Ignatius

200

Dixon

Ravalli

Jocko River

N

Flathead River

are prohibited on the entire lower Flathead during the waterfowl nesting season (March 15-June 30). Motors larger than 15 horsepower are prohibited at all times.

The lower Flathead has the dubious distinction of being perhaps the worst trout fishing stream of its size in western Montana. Fisheries studies have discovered only 15 trout per mile on the average, with many stretches much lower. It is believed the irregular fluctuations of Kerr Dam may make spawning habitat inaccessible; the glacial silts found in the river are also thought to contribute to poor fish productivity. Be sure to check the fishing regulations, as this section recently switched to catch-and-release (catch them if you can!) trout fishing.

But before you decide to leave your fishing rod at home, think again. The lower Flathead has an outstanding and extraordinary northern-pike fishery that more than compensates for the trout scarcity. Fisheries biologists report that the *average* pike caught in the Flathead weighs about 7 pounds, and that pike in the 20-pound class are not at all unusual. The northerns were introduced at Lone Pine Reservoir about 20 years ago, and then made their way to the Flathead via the Little Bitterroot River. The basic technique is to fish the shallow, weedy backwater areas of the river with either smelt or large red and white dardevles—hang on tight!

The lower Flathead has four major access points: Buffalo Bridge, Sloan Bridge, Dixon, and Perma. The 22-mile section between Buffalo Bridge and Sloan Bridge receives the most pressure. While this trip can be made in a day (get an early start), some people prefer to go overnight and continue to Dixon, the next access point.

The section of the river between Dixon and Perma receives little pressure from floaters, but it's used by motorboaters. Conversely, the river above Sloan Bridge receives minimal motorboat use.

Although the lower Flathead has some frisky riffles, it's an easy float beginners can enjoy—the type of trip where one can play a guitar or eat a picnic lunch while watching the scenery pass by. But keep an eye peeled for occasional rocks or other obstructions.

Canoes probably do best on this big river, as strong headwinds sometimes cause problems for rafts. Under normal conditions, however, almost any craft will do.

If you go overnight, take water, as the river isn't suitable for drinking. Keep in mind that most of the river flows through the Flathead Indian Reservation, and floaters between the ages of 18 (there has been a proposal to drop the lower age to 12) and 65 need a tribal recreational use permit.

The lower Flathead is another river which the Corps of Engineers haunts. They're currently eyeing at least six possible dam sites. The Corps' proposals have been stomped on and torn apart by local citizens as well as the Confederated Salish and Kootenai Tribes. Such proposals are like a fungus. While you're never really sure whether they're dead or alive, you just can't kill them. Watch for further developments.

The Middle Fork of the Flathead River

Those who have floated the Middle Fork of the Flathead know why it's called Montana's wildest river. Numerous large boulders have settled in the bottom of this heavily glaciated valley, which drops an average of 35 feet per mile as it plunges out of the largest expanse of wilderness in the lower 48 states. Downed trees partially blockade the river, creating serious hazards for floaters but excellent habitat for fish. Throw in the highly variable water flows, and the Middle Fork is plainly not a stream for the faint-hearted.

A designated component of the National Wild and Scenic Rivers System, the tumultuous Middle Fork gets its start high in the undisturbed peaks of the Bob Marshall Wilderness. As Dale Burk explains in his book, *Great Bear, Wild River*, "The

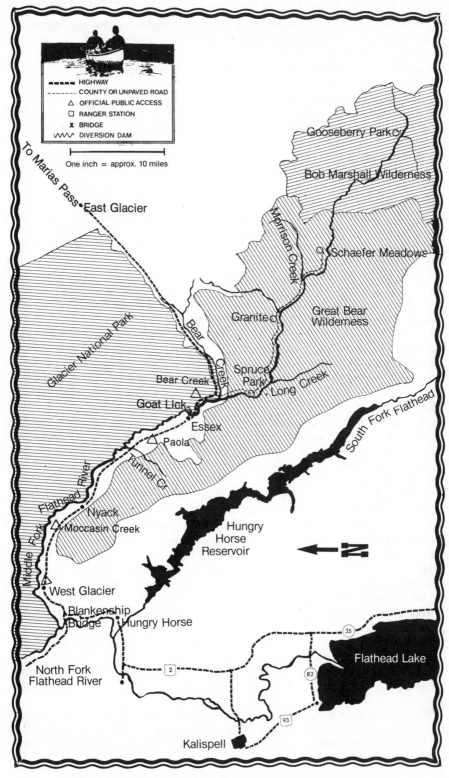

Middle Fork of the Flathead River

Middle Fork of the Flathead begins hard against the Continental Divide in the steep, highly erosive slopes of mountains where a glacier once rode the earth. . . . It is set amidst startlingly scenic mountains, its channel often literally carved through the sedimentary rock cliffs that sweep straight upward onto slopes so steep they are difficult for a man to hike upon.'

Burk's book chronicles the bitterly fought battle to establish the Great Bear Wilderness. The Great Bear, named for the grizzlies which inhabit the area, was designated wilderness in 1978. This 285,000-acre area encompasses nearly 50 miles of the Middle Fork.

The uppermost sections of the Middle Fork are very inaccessible, only reached by foot or horse. A pack trail parallels the river for most of its wilderness flow, and outfitters often take people in for this grand sight.

Despite its remote location, the most common access to the wilderness section of the river is by airplane via Schaefer Meadows. This airstrip and Forest Service guard station are about 25 miles upstream from Bear Creek, where the river meets civilization. For the remaining 35 miles, U.S. 2 parallels the Middle Fork, and forms the south border of Glacier National Park.

The waters of the Middle Fork rise dramatically when the snow melts. Although the river usually carries only about 900 cubic feet per second (cfs) of water in February, this level may climb to over 11,000 cfs in May, when peak flows usually occur. The river may be unfloatable during the peak discharge.

The optimum floating period on the Middle Fork is usually between early June and mid-July. Since river flows come directly from melting snowbanks, air temperatures often dictate float conditions. Keep in mind, however, that June water temperatures will usually stay around 40 degrees, regardless of air temperature. Rainstorms, combined with the low water temperatures, make hypothermia a real threat on early-season floats.

After about mid-July, the flows in the upper stretches drop sharply, and floating often becomes impossible. In low water, each rapid becomes a maze of exposed rocks that can slice rafts beyond repair. Check river conditions with the Forest Service's Hungry Horse Ranger District at Hungry Horse.

When the river is ripping and roaring, it's easy to float from Schaefer Meadows to Bear Creek in a day. Most floaters, however, choose to take a couple of days to explore the Great Bear. Those who go overnight usually go past Bear Creek and take out at the highway bridge near Essex. With these few extra miles, floaters not only catch a couple more good rapids, but they also get to visit the famous goat lick on the edge of Glacier Park.

The goat lick is a slumping cliff on the north side of the river where mountain goats come down from the crags to lick exposed mineral salts. It's one of the few places in North America where one can view wild goats next to a wild river. If you've managed to keep your camera dry, it's an excellent place to take pictures. Don't approach the goats too closely.

The trip through the wilderness section of the Middle Fork can be run by intermediates when the water is normal, but only by experts when it's high. The rapids change from year to year as boulders tumble into the river and trees lodge in different places. The most difficult rapids lie in a three-mile canyon below Spruce Park (see white-water section).

The remoteness of the upper Middle Fork makes it doubly dangerous. If you have had little experience in running white-water rivers as technically difficult as the Middle Fork, think twice before trying it on your own. Several commercial outfitters work

Grizzly bear, namesake of the Great Bear Wilderness. Doug O'looney photo.

the upper river; their names can be obtained from the Hungry Horse Ranger District.

Not only does the Middle Fork require considerable skill, but it also demands quality equipment. A durable raft with a rowing platform is the standard. For safety purposes, it's best to have two rafts per party. Be sure to take along extra paddles or oars, as they can be snapped off on cliff walls or submerged logs. Wetsuits or rain gear are recommended, and don't forget bailing buckets. This is one river where

Small drop on the Middle Fork of the Flathead River. Hugh Zackheim photo.

it's not necessary to remind people to wear life jackets; you may wish you had two.

The wilderness trip on the Middle Fork becomes more popular each year. The Forest Service has placed restrictions on the numbers of commercial outfitters. Other than that, the only other restriction is a maximum party size of 10 for both commercial and non-commercial groups.

This area has obvious potential for overuse, so tread as lightly as possible on this designated wilderness. The steepness of the terrain restricts the number of campsites, which usually can be found near where tributaries enter; try to avoid the Cascade Creek campsite, as it gets very heavily used. Because of the grizzlies in the area, be careful about storing your food and keeping a clean campsite.

The nonwilderness section of the river also has some extremely challenging water (see white-water section). The section of river between Bear Creek and Essex contains some tricky rapids and big waves. Expert or strong intermediate canoeists sometimes challenge the Middle Fork between Tunnel Creek and Nyack, but be prepared to bail water. Occasional logjams can make it dangerous.

After Nyack comes the John Stevens Canyon, a very popular white-water section. It's a narrow canyon with almost continuous white water, suitable for intermediates or experts, depending on water levels. It's popular with rafters as well as kayakers.

Near West Glacier, the Middle Fork widens and slows down. From West Glacier to the Blankenship Bridge is a good, half-day float for beginners in rafts or canoes.

The nonwilderness section of the Middle Fork receives heavy summertime use, much of it from Glacier Park visitors. At least five different commercial outfitters work the river.

The tourists usually get their money's worth, as moose, deer, bears, and a host of smaller mammals and birds often can be seen near the river. Cutthroat trout, bull trout, and whitefish—all native fish—fin through the waters and occasionally fall prey to artificial flies or wobbling spoons. Kokanee salmon are abundant in the river in October when they migrate from Flathead Lake to spawn.

Appropriately, the Middle Fork of the Flathead is one of the best protected rivers in Montana: it's a designated "wild" river for nearly half its length, its headwaters are in the Bob Marshall Wilderness, it flows through the Great Bear Wilderness, and it borders Glacier Park. The biggest threat comes from people. So far, the Forest Service has done a good job of managing people problems. Let them know if you run into problems which you feel they should address.

The North Fork of the Flathead River

Born of glacial torrents, the North Fork of the Flathead flows wild and pure out of Canada and then gushes southward 58 miles in Montana, forming the west boundary of Glacier National Park. This beautiful, limpid-green river joins the Middle Fork of the Flathead near Blankenship Bridge to form the main trunk of the Flathead. The entire length of the North Fork is a designated part of the National Wild and Scenic Rivers System. All of the North Fork country is an elegant blend of towering mountains, verdant forests, and sparkling waters.

Considering the North Fork's near-wilderness setting, access is quite good. Although undeveloped roads parallel the river for its entire distance in Montana, they rarely can be seen. The controversial North Fork Road runs along the west side of the river. Some folks want the road improved to promote tourism and logging; conservationists and most local residents want it left the way it is—bumpy and narrow. So far the bumpy-road folks have prevailed.

On the east side of the river in Glacier Park, an undeveloped road (often called the "inside" North Fork Road), that leads to Kintla Lake offers limited river access. Boats can be launched east of the river from Polebridge and the Riverfront Campground, located about four miles north of Poleridge.

Most floaters prefer to launch from the west side of the river. Developed river access points, from north to south, include the Canadian border, Ford River, Big Creek, Glacier Rim, and Blankenship Bridge. There's an undeveloped launch site next to the county road at Polebridge; this site is midway between the Ford River access and Big Creek.

In 1892, a steamboat attempted to ascend the North Fork. This ill-fated trip was conceived by an enterprising man by the name of James Talbot. Talbot, an early-day boomer, learned of the coal deposits along the North Fork and conceived the idea of using this coal to induce the construction of a railroad, which would bless his town of Columbia Falls and greatly stimulate the development of the entire region.

Talbot had a 75-foot steamship built, named it *The Oakes,* and in May of 1892 attempted the swollen North Fork. After several days of hard work, the crew was only 15 miles upriver. It was at this point that the steamer *Oakes* hit a difficult rapid which sunk her. Though none of the crew was lost, they all had to traverse difficult terrain to make their way back to Columbia Falls.

While steamships no longer try the North Fork, an armada of rafters and canoeists challenge it each year. Fortunately, the floating pressure is fairly well-distributed; the section from Ford to Big Creek probably gets used more than any other.

Floating in Montana begins at the Canadian border river access and continues for the North Fork's entire distance in Montana. From the Canadian border to Polebridge, the river is suitable for intermediates. Numerous logjams and fast currents will pro-

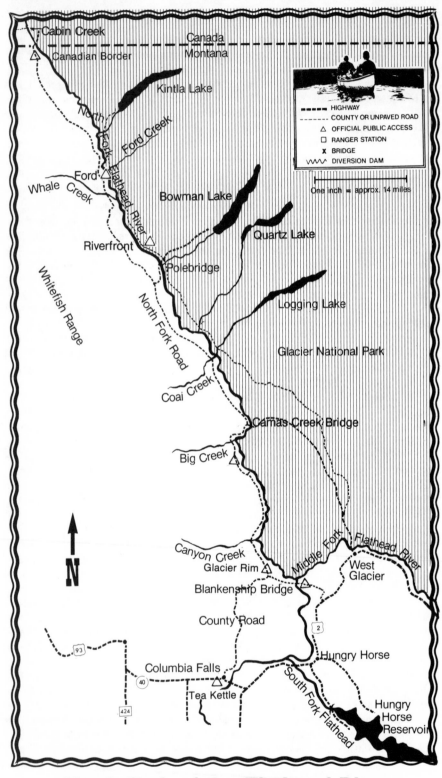

North Fork of the Flathead River

vide some adventure, particularly when the water is high. Runoff sometimes lasts well into July.

The easiest section of the river lies between Polebridge and Big Creek. Beginners can handle it when the water is low and weather conditions are favorable, but should stay clear during runoff. The North Fork has extremely cold water, and early-season spills can be very dangerous. Again, watch carefully for logjams and narrow channels. Be wary of shallow riffles where the current is fast; these can tip your canoe if you aren't parallel to the current. Be prepared to jump out in shallow spots if you get hung up.

The toughest section of the North Fork lies between Big Creek and the Glacier Rim River access. Logjams are very common, and there are some troublesome high waves. The most challenging water, known as the Fool Hen Rapids, lies about two miles upstream from Canyon Creek. During high water, it takes an expert to negotiate the occasional rocks and tricky currents if he's using an open canoe. In fact, many experts don't make it through right-side-up. Intermediate rafters should have little trouble, and it's relatively easy for kayakers.

Spring runoff on the North Fork usually starts in late May and runs through late June. Best conditions are usually from about mid-July to mid-August. After mid-August, particularly during dry years, the river from the border to Ford can get too low to float. From Ford downriver, the North Fork is usually floatable unless it's frozen. Fall trips can be outstanding when there's enough water. Get up-to-date information by calling the Forest Service's Glacier View Ranger District in Columbia Falls at (406) 892-4372.

Fishing on the North Fork is often mediocre, but it's unpredictable. Most of the fish in the river are migratory, so you have to be there at the right time, often in late summer.

The North Fork is one of the few remaining rivers in Montana that supports a native fishery. The two primary species are the westslope cutthroat (also known as the Montana black-spotted trout) and the Dolly Varden or bull trout. The Dolly Varden gets its name from a female character in a Charles Dicken's novel who always dressed in gaudy clothes. A number of the char family, the beautifully colored Dolly Varden lives up to its name. These fish, which were once native to many Montana rivers, are now found in significant numbers only in the forks of the Flathead. Some feel they could become a candidate for the federal endangered species list.

The North Fork is very much a glacial stream and doesn't have the nutrients which make the southwestern trout streams so productive. As a result, there are fewer fish and they grow more slowly. The cutthroat trout has justifiably earned the title of being the stupidest fish that swims, another factor that makes the North Fork a river where overfishing can be a problem. It's a good place for catch-and-release fishing—especially for the larger fish.

Look carefully for wildlife while paddling down the North Fork. Its proximity to Glacier Park, along with its own natural values, makes it an ideal spot to see many wild critters. Bald eagles and osprey are common, as are the moose which prefer the willow bottoms. Some floaters have even sighted grizzly bears or otters along the river.

While the North Fork presently runs clean and pure, several threats make the future cloudy. High-grade coal underlies much of the river's headwaters in Canada, and a coal company has been studying the feasibility of open-pit mining near Cabin Creek, a tributary of the North Fork just eight miles over the border.

If possible coal development isn't enough, much of the surrounding Flathead National Forest is being explored for oil and gas. Tag on to that serious subdivisions problems and extensive logging throughout the North Fork drainage, and it's easy to see

Canoe race on Fool Hen Rapids, North Fork of the Flathead.
Mark O'hearn photo.

why so many citizens are concerned about this wild river.

A group of citizens known as the North Fork Preservation Association has formed to make sure that development in the North Fork drainage doesn't destroy the natural values of the river. If you'd like to see the North Fork remain wild, you would do well to roll up your sleeves and take up the cause before it's too late. The association's address is Box 4, Polebridge, MT 59928.

The South Fork of the Flathead River

Edwin Way Teale once wrote, "To the lost man, to the pioneer penetrating a new country, to the naturalist who wishes to see the wild land at its wildest, the advice is always the same—follow a river. The river is the original forest highway. It is nature's own Wilderness Road." So it is with the South Fork of the Flathead River, the main travel route through the Bob Marshall Wilderness. The South Fork is probably Montana's most pristine and inaccessible river. It's a designated component of the national Wild and Scenic Rivers System.

Those wishing to float the "wild" section of the South Fork have to hike or ride horses a considerable distance before they hit the water. Most people approach the South Fork via Holland Lake and Gordon Creek, a distance of about 27 miles. Others pack in over Pyramid Pass and reach the South Fork via Youngs Creek, which is slightly longer. The usual starting point is Big Prairie, as the river is sometimes too low for floating after mid-July above this point.

The wilderness trip from Big Prairie to Spotted Bear Ranger Station covers about 45 miles and can easily be floated in four days. Because of the long haul in, most people make the trip in four or six-person rafts, two persons and 60 pounds of gear per raft. Campsites are easy to find along the river.

From Big Prairie to Salmon Forks, a distance of about 15 miles, you can relax and enjoy the scenery, as there are few or no rapids. This upper section of the river may have logjams that completely block the river, however, making portages necessary. This upper portion can get rather shallow by late summer, and it may be necessary to drag your raft across the riffles. Salmon Forks can generally be reached the first day.

The next section between Salmon Forks and Black Bear Creek is about 12 miles. Here, the river increases in depth and begins to form more pools and riffles. The South Fork's water is extraordinarily clear and pure, and the bottom is dotted with brick-red, chalk-white and aqua-green rocks. The water is so clear that with polarized sunglasses,

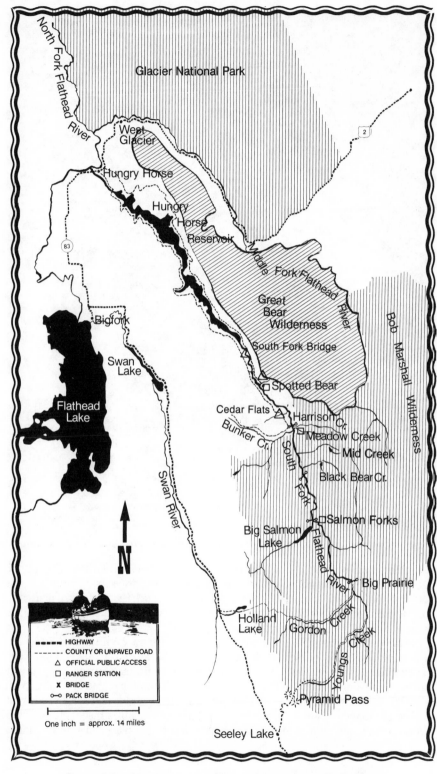

North Fork Flathead River

Glacier National Park

West Glacier

Hungry Horse

Hungry Horse Reservoir

83

Bigfork

Swan Lake

Flathead Lake

Whale Fork Flathead River

Great Bear Wilderness

South Fork Bridge

Bob Marshall Wilderness

Spotted Bear

Cedar Flats

Bunker Cr.

Harrison Cr.

Meadow Creek

Mid Creek

Black Bear Cr.

South Fork

Salmon Forks

Big Salmon Lake

Flathead River

Big Prairie

Swan River

Gordon Creek

Holland Lake

Youngs Creek

Pyramid Pass

N

▬▬▬ HIGHWAY
------ COUNTY OR UNPAVED ROAD
△ OFFICIAL PUBLIC ACCESS
☐ RANGER STATION
✕ BRIDGE
⊶ PACK BRIDGE

One inch = approx. 14 miles

Seeley Lake

South Fork of the Flathead River

A narrow restriction on the South Fork—this is the entire river. Carol Fischer photo.

it's often possible to see a trout coming to a fly well before it strikes. Fishing for cutthroat trout is excellent in this section. While the river speeds up a bit, it's still not too difficult. What's so remarkable about the South Fork isn't that it's so unusually spectacular, but that it's so wild and untrammeled—it looks much like many other western Montana valleys, except it has no roads.

Floaters usually hit the tough part of the South Fork on the third day. While it's only about nine river miles from Black Bear Creek to Harrison Creek, allow an entire day for this spectacular section. The hazards begin in a narrow canyon just downstream from where Mid Creek pours into the South Fork. A large Forest Service sign just above this point warns boaters this is the last safe takeout if you intend to portage around the gorge. In the course of the next two miles below the sign, the river squeezes into restrictions so narrow in two separate places that a raft cannot pass through. At one of these points, it's possible to stand with one foot on each side of the river and watch the river flow between your legs.

Less than a mile below the second major restriction comes the incredible Meadow Creek gorge. Be prepared for a spectacular entry. Just above the gorge, there's a tricky little rapid that shoots you around a blind corner, under the Meadow Creek packbridge and into the gorge. It's a real thrill, as the river is too fast and the cliff walls too steep to permit any inspection of the river. Instead, you blast into the gorge hoping there aren't any serious obstacles.

From a sheerly geologic perspective, the gorge is clearly the most spectacular part of the trip. Canyon walls rise up nearly 150 feet, as the gorge itself is but a narrow cleft, a ribbon of water in an otherwise solid mass of rock. Often less than 15 feet wide, it's like being in a labyrinth, as the canyon twists and turns and it's impossible to see what lies around the corner. It's quite dark in the bottom of the canyon, and eerily quiet except for one place where a waterfall pounds down. While the current in the mile-long gorge is rather swift, it's smooth and there aren't any real hazards. While winding around the curves, however, one can't help but be apprehensive about the possibility of a logjam in this narrow chasm. In some places it's possible to look up to the top and see logs that completely bridge the canyon. For the gorge and other parts of the canyon as well, you'll want to have a stout stick or a canoe paddle handy to keep your boat from bouncing off the walls; it's often so narrow it's impossible to use a basic eight-foot oar.

Immediately past the gorge begins the most difficult white water of the river. Large rocks in the swift current make passage rather technical, and extensive scouting is recommended. The white water doesn't last very long, however, and by the time Harrison Creek enters, the difficult water is behind.

The last part of the wilderness portion of the South Fork—from Harrison Creek to Spotted Bear—may well be the wildest and most beautiful of all. It's certainly the most isolated. While the upper section of the river receives fairly heavy use because of outfitters, the outfitters don't take clients through the gorge, and consequently the river below Mid Creek is only lightly used. The only access points are the Meadow Creek airstrip or the Cedar Flats river access, off the Meadow Creek Road. The Cedar Flats access involves a short hike down to the river, but it is possible to carry a boat down.

From Spotted Bear down to where the river is impounded by Hungry Horse Reservoir, there's easy public access and the river isn't difficult. Beware in high water, however.

While most of the South Fork isn't difficult at all, the incredible isolation of this river makes it far too risky for beginners. Errors here can mean serious discomfort or even death. Intermediates could make the trip if they portage around the hazardous section, which is a little over four miles by trail.

Only experts should attempt to float through the hazardous section between Mid Creek and Harrison Creek. While the gorge itself is not technically that dangerous, the hazard level is high and there's little margin for error. Anyone floating below the warning sign should get out and scout each dangerous point. It's always possible to get out and scout except where the river rushes under the Meadow Creek pack bridge. Don't worry about getting swept into one of the hazards—you'll hear the roar well in advance. There are two points where a portage is mandatory because of the narrow restrictions; the portage routes are obvious along the canyon walls and only require a short carry. There's one other narrow point—with a sharp rock at the bottom of the rapid—which you may want to line your boat around.

Few people risk the South Fork during runoff which usually peaks in mid-June.

July is the prime-time floating season for the South Fork; in dry years it gets too low by mid-August. Contact the Forest Service's Spotted Bear Ranger Station for South Fork water-level information.

Anyone floating the South Fork should have quality equipment, as a cheap raft won't withstand the punishment this river can dish out. Be sure to take a patch kit as well as a spare paddle. Because of the narrowness of this river, small rafts with two people per boat work best. Also, short oars will work better than long ones because there are so many tight spots.

The Gallatin River

The Gallatin River springs from the snow-clad peaks of the Madison and Gallatin mountain ranges, and it courses for more than 90 miles before joining the Madison and Jefferson rivers at Three Forks. The Gallatin comes close to being an alpine stream as it spills through the scenic Gallatin Canyon, where frequent rapids alternate with deep, green pools alive with trout.

Lewis and Clark named the Gallatin for President Jefferson's Secretary of the Treasury. Despite a great deal of development, the Gallatin remains one of the most lovely valleys in Montana. The Indians knew this area as "the valley of the flowers."

It's also an area steeped in history, much of it made by an adventurous man from Georgia named John Bozeman. He blazed a trail through the Gallatin that started in Fort Laramie, Wyoming, and ended at the gold fields near Virginia City, Montana. His trail, known as the Bozeman or Bonanza Trail, was shorter than other routes, but it cut across Indian hunting grounds protected by treaty. Development of this trail caused much hostility among the Indians, and many settlers, soldiers, and Indians died along the route. Bozeman himself was killed by the Blackfeet in 1867, and the trail closed shortly thereafter.

Lewis and Clark also explored the Gallatin Valley and found it much to their liking. On July 14, 1806, on the return trip from the Pacific, Captain Clark wrote in his journal, "I saw Elk, Deer and Antelope, and great deal of old signs of buffalo. Their roads is in every direction . . . emence quantities of beaver on this Fork . . . and their dams very much impede the navigation of it."

Had Captain Clark proceeded very far upstream, he would have noted that treacherous rapids also impede navigation. These rapids would have sorely tested the Corps of Discovery's buffalo-skin boats. Modern-day explorers, however, find the white water much to their liking (see white-water section).

The Gallatin River actually consists of two forks, the East Gallatin and the West Gallatin rivers. Because the West Gallatin is substantially larger, it's generally recognized as the mainstem Gallatin. While both branches are floatable, they differ sharply in character. The East Gallatin is a winding meadow stream that once had an outstanding fishery, then experienced some serious pollution problems, and is now on the rebound. The West Gallatin, on the other hand, is a swift stream noted for its good fishing and outstanding white-water boating.

The sinuous East Gallatin has the brushy banks and high nutrients that often make a good fishery. Until the mid-1960s, trout up to 10 pounds were common, and Department of Fish, Wildlife and Parks biologists recorded one brown trout that weighed 17 pounds and measured 36 inches.

In 1965, however, the Bozeman municipal sewage plant (located just below the Springhill Road bridge) went into operation, destroying the fishery for about 10 miles downstream and severely impacting the rest of the stream. Since that time, improvements have allowed trout populations to recover, although the river still has sedimentation problems. Streamside brush removal and some channelization have also destroyed fish habitat on the East Gallatin, but good fishing can be found where the banks remain intact.

Floating on the East Gallatin varies directly with water flows. Most of the East Gallatin, with the exception of the portion below Dry Creek, gets too low for floating by midsummer. Early in the season, floating is possible as high as the Springhill Road bridge. This winding upper section, which has numerous barbed wire fences across it, can be handled by intermediate canoeists; rafters may have trouble. Below Dry Creek, beginners can give it a try, although the sharp bends and occasional brush piles will necessitate constant maneuvering. Because the river is so narrow and winding, it's rather difficult to float, but some people do because the access is difficult otherwise.

Access to the East Gallatin is provided by county-road bridges, which usually are about five miles apart; there are few official access points. Most of the river receives only moderate floating pressure.

The West Gallatin receives most of the attention, and for good reason. After its start in Yellowstone Park the West Gallatin dashes its way through beautiful forested country.

The West Gallatin is strictly for experienced floaters. From Taylor Fork to the West Fork, intermediate canoeists and rafters can test their skills. During peak flows, however, canoeists will likely have problems with high waves.

Below the West Fork, the Gallatin becomes extremely difficult all the way to Squaw Creek, and only experts or solid intermediates should challenge it. The most difficult section of all is a two-mile run directly below the highway bridge at Cascade Creek. Best reserved for the experts, large rocks in the river spawn tricky currents and frothing water.

The famed House Rock rapids, the most formidable of all, are visible from the highway, and crowds often gather to watch the intrepid boaters. At peak flows, only floaters with high-flotation life jackets and wet suits should try this.

The excellent access along the upper reaches of the West Gallatin contributes to its popularity. Most of the white-water fun takes place in May and June, as the water generally gets low after mid-July.

Although the West Gallatin loses its white water below the mouth of the Gallatin

Beginners can forget the West Gallatin River. Doug O'looney photo.

Elk, common in the Gallatin Valley. Harry Engels photo.

Canyon, it remains difficult until it reaches the East Gallatin near Manhattan. The river frequently channels and has numerous logjams that sometimes completely block the river. Numerous diversion dams, which move water to the rich agricultural lands, also create serious hazards. Rafters are smart to pass up this section. Only expert canoeists or kayakers should try it during runoff. Afterwards, intermediates can handle it if there's enough water. Irrigation dewatering may deter summer floating in some sections.

The West Gallatin, particularly from the mouth of the canyon to Gallatin Gateway, sustains a notable trout fishery. Biologists report trout populations of fish 10 inches or larger at more than 1,300 fish per mile. While it's not reknowned for large trout, fish in the three- to five-pound range are caught each year. Boaters should be aware that the entire West Gallatin—from Yellowstone Park to its confluence with the East

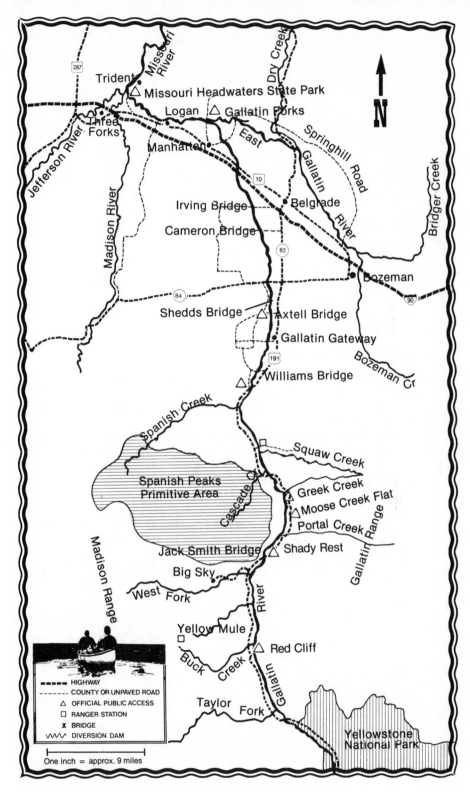

Gallatin River

Gallatin—is closed to float-fishing. The closure is designed to alleviate conflicts between floaters and bank fishermen.

The two forks of the Gallatin join about two miles north of Manhattan (near Gallatin Forks fishing access site) and provide easy floating suitable for beginners as far as the Lyman Bridge near Logan, about five miles downstream. From Logan to Trident, another five miles downstream, occasional logjams and sharp bends make this section trickier. Like the lower sections of the Jefferson and Madison, this last stretch is alive with wildlife, including waterfowl, deer, and moose.

The Gallatin River is just beginning to feel the full impact of man-caused pollution. A recent federal report identified four problem areas:

• Logging and construction activities in geologically fragile areas (such as Yellow Mules and Buck Creek), causing sediment pollution of both forks through their tributaries.

• Agricultural practices (including brush removal and overgrazing) in the valley, resulting in sedimentation and erosion.

• Pollution of ground water in the valley caused by a dramatic increase in the number of underground sewage systems being installed.

• Urban runoff as well as discharges from Bozeman's sewage treatment facility, which hurt the fishery in East Gallatin.

The problems have been identified, and it will take innovative thinkers to discover and attain the solutions.

The Jefferson River

For those who like to drift back in history as they float down rivers, the Jefferson offers a gold mine of river lore. Not only did Lewis and Clark travel its entire length, but the famous mountain man John Colter also made his legendary run along the Jefferson's brushy banks.

In the spring of 1808, Colter and a companion were each paddling a canoe down the Jefferson when they were accosted by Blackfeet Indians, a tribe vigorously resisting the invasion of the white man. The Indians motioned for them to come to shore. Colter's companion balked, which was a fatal mistake; he was killed on the spot and Colter was captured.

Since Colter's scalp was a substantial prize, the Indians decided it would go to the fleetest brave. Colter was stripped of his clothes and shoes and told he would be given a chance to run for his life. When the chief inquired about the white man's speed, the clever Colter responded he was a poor runner. For that reason, the Indians gave Colter a head start—all the speedy fur trapper needed. He ran about five miles before diving into the river and finding a hiding spot under a logjam. Although the Indians searched the river extensively, they failed to find the well-hidden mountain man.

Colter's ordeal, however, had only begun. When night fell, he began the long trek to nearest civilization—a fort at the mouth of the Bighorn River, 250 miles east. Without food or clothing, he reportedly covered the distance in 11 days, losing so much weight in the process that his friends didn't recognize him when he appeared at the fort.

The Beaverhead and Big Hole rivers merge near Twin Bridges to form the Jefferson, which then flows generally northeast for about 60 miles. The river winds and braids repeatedly through mostly arid benchland and irrigated farmland. It encompasses a wide band of thick, brushy riverbottom.

Captain Lewis' August 2, 1805, description of the Jefferson River and its valley remains quite accurate today. His journal reads: "we found the current very rapid waist deep and about 90 yds. wide. bottom smooth pebble with a small mixture of coarse

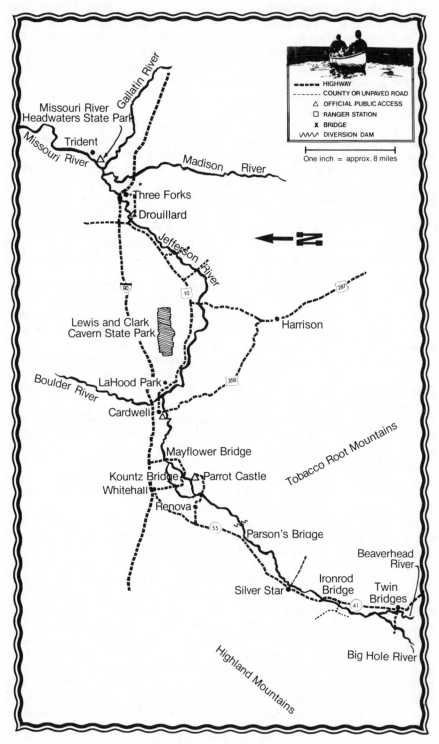

Gallatin River

Missouri River
Headwaters State Park

Missouri River

Trident

Madison River

Three Forks

Drouillard

Jefferson River

N

90

10

287

Lewis and Clark
Cavern State Park

Harrison

Boulder River

LaHood Park

359

Cardwell

Tobacco Root Mountains

Mayflower Bridge

Kountz Bridge   △ Parrot Castle

Whitehall

Renova

55

Parson's Bridge

Beaverhead
River

Ironrod
Bridge

Twin
Bridges

Silver Star

41

Highland Mountains

Big Hole River

Jefferson River

gravel . . . The valley along which we passed today, and through which the river winds it's meandering course is from 6 to 8 miles wide and consists of a beautifull level plain with but little timber, and that confined to the verge of the river; the land is tolerably fertile, and is either black or dark yellow loam, covered with grass from 9 inches to 2 feet high. the plain ascends gradually on either side of the river to the bases of two ranges of high mountains. the tops of these mountains are yet covered partially with snow, while we in the valley are nearly suffocated with the intense heat of the mid-day sun; the nights are so cold that two blankets are not more than sufficient covering.''

The Corps of Discovery had an arduous journey as they lined their boats up the brushy-banked and swift-moving Jefferson. Hot weather, mosquitoes, and slippery rocks also plagued the crew. Today, modern explorers encounter some of the same problems.

Captain Lewis even got lost on the Jefferson and was forced to sleep for the evening on an island. During his restless night, he heard a large splash which he feared was the dreaded "white" bear, the grizzly. River rats no longer have to deal with Old Griz.

River explorers will be pleased to find parts of the Jefferson much as Lewis and Clark saw it. The picturesque Tobacco Root Mountains (still largely unroaded) rise to the east of the river, while the more rounded Highland Mountains enliven the view on the west side. Most of the riverbottom remains undeveloped, although cattle have replaced the elk Lewis and Clark saw.

Water quality is the biggest change since frontier days. Irrigation runoff and grazing practices produce sediment that often clouds the Jefferson's waters. Although the Jefferson is usually clear in late summer and fall, rainstorms can muddy the river in short order. In addition, excessive nutrients in the water often foster rapid growth of algae in the summer. This can be a nuisance for anglers and swimmers.

If you fish the Jefferson when conditions are right, the rewards can be substantial. Some anglers report taking—and releasing—over 100 brown trout in a day. Here's a substantiated report, however; on my last trip down the Jefferson, I caught only two undersized trout. Water clarity and temperature are critical for successful fly fishing. Most fishermen favor big wet flies or streamers for the Jefferson. Rainbows and a few cutthroat inhabit the river along with browns and many whitefish. The Jefferson is usually open all year for fishing.

A topic fisheries biologists have jawed about over a campfire is what the Jefferson might be like if smallmouth bass were introduced. Some people think the habitat is ideal and an outstanding fishery would develop. Others think introduction of non-native fish is a bad idea. It's interesting to ponder.

With proper caution, the entire Jefferson can be floated by beginners. Much of the river is broad and slow-moving, although the river often channels and picks up some speed. Logjams, protruding trees, and narrow channels are the major hazards.

In the upper sections, the river is quite removed from civilization. Occasional diversions and riprap, however, will remind you that man isn't far away. Near the Ironrod Bridge, watch carefully for diversion dams; the diversion below Parson's Bridge is also hazardous. This area is often seriously dewatered in the summer, and floating may not be possible. Adequate instream flows to protect fish and wildlife are sorely needed.

Below the Renova Bridge, the river divides into two channels of nearly equal size for about eight miles, forming a large island. This section of the river is particularly scenic as it sweeps by the Tobacco Roots. Directly below LaHood Park, the river enters a narrow canyon, as does the old highway, which parallels the river for the next several miles. As the river cuts through the canyon, it forms many deep pools as well as a few fast runs. Steep limestone walls and colorful rock formations make it an interesting section. The well-known Lewis and Clark Caverns—which were never actually visited by Lewis and Clark—can be viewed from the river just a few miles below Cardwell.

As the river approaches Three Forks, it again becomes isolated. It braids into several channels as it winds through brushy, lowland habitat for its last few miles before helping to form the Missouri. The numerous channel changes and occasional downed trees make this the trickiest section. Still, beginners can handle it if the water isn't high.

This last few miles of the Jefferson is one of the best sections for seeing wildlife. Ducks and geese nest in this area, and the brush is alive with whitetails. The area also has a good moose population, so keep your eyes peeled for the king of the deer family.

The Jefferson receives a fair amount of floating pressure, but it seems to be well-distributed. Most floaters are fishermen from Butte. Popular access points include Parrot Castle, Cardwell, Williams Bridge and Drouilliard fishing access sites, Ironrod Bridge at Silver Star, and Three Forks.

The Kootenai River

The Kootenai rises in British Columbia and flows southwest in a great loop through northwestern Montana. The river's total length is more than 480 miles; in volume, it's the second largest river in Montana. "Kootenai" is an Indian word meaning "deer robes."

The first white man to navigate the Kootenai was David Thompson, who paddled

The beaver, the Corps of Engineers' mascot, is common along the Kootenai and most other Montana rivers. Dick Randall photo.

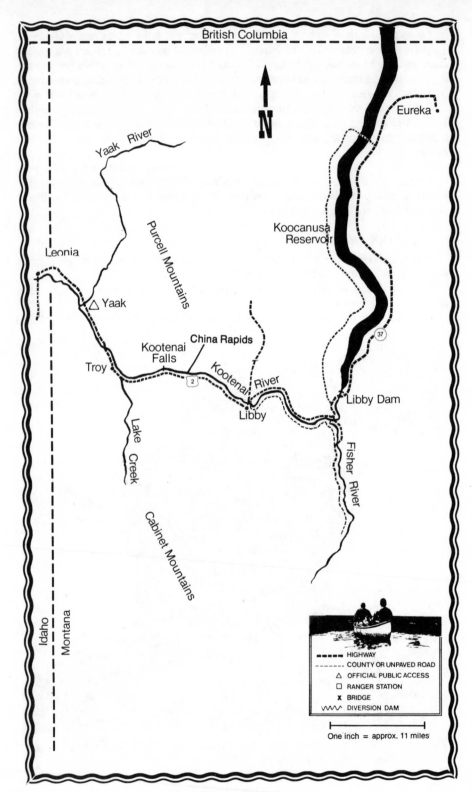

British Columbia

N

Yaak River

Leonia

Purcell Mountains

△ Yaak

Koocanusa Reservoir

Kootenai Falls

China Rapids

Troy

Kootenai River

Libby

Libby Dam

Lake Creek

Fisher River

Cabinet Mountains

Idaho

Montana

HIGHWAY
COUNTY OR UNPAVED ROAD
△ OFFICIAL PUBLIC ACCESS
□ RANGER STATION
X BRIDGE
〜〜〜 DIVERSION DAM

One inch = approx. 11 miles

Kootenai River

a birch-bark canoe down the river in 1808 and later founded a settlement near Libby. The river has an interesting history; even steamboats traveled on it for a short time while the mining industry was booming.

Floating on the Kootenai starts below Libby Dam and continues to the Idaho border and beyond. Although most local folks prefer small aluminum boats, canoes and rafts also work well. While most of the river is broad and swift-flowing, occasional rapids and high waves call for caution. Because of the great fluctuations in the amount of water discharged from Koocanusa Reservoir (resulting in changes of two to four feet in river levels), conditions can vary widely. Because of the fluctuations and occasional rapids, beginners should steer clear of the Kootenai above the falls.

Below Libby, as the river approaches Kootenai Falls, there's some difficult water known as China Rapids. As the story goes, the rapids got their name in the 1860s when a party of Chinese miners from British Columbia tried to raft down the river with a load of gold dust. They took the river rather than an overland route because they feared their fortune would be stolen by white miners. As the raft hit the rapids, however, the heavy gold shifted and the raft upended. Only one miner made it to shore to tell the story, and the river kept the gold.

All but the very best canoeists (with or without gold) should portage around China Rapids. Intermediate rafters and kayakers can try it, but be sure to scout it first.

The power line above Kootenai Falls marks a good takeout point for floaters. Don't worry about missing the power line; you'll see and hear the falls in plenty of time. Obviously, floaters should be careful not to venture too close to the falls. Early settlers called it "Disaster Falls" for good reason.

Immediately below the falls the river remains fast and turbulent for about two miles. Only experts in kayaks and large rafts should try it. Don't forget that the extreme water fluctuations caused by the dam make this section different each time. Each of the five major rapids in this two-mile gorge should be inspected on foot before going through.

Below Troy, as the river leaves the highway, lies the last Montana vestige of the Kootenai as it once was. Although railroad tracks parallel the river, one can still get a feeling of isolation on this big river, particularly below where the Yaak River enters.

While the transparent Kootenai remains large and fast-flowing, beginners can handle it with caution. High waves create the biggest hazard, and they can swamp open canoes. Most of the choppy water can be skirted if it's seen in time. The worst high waves in the lower section are right where the Yaak River enters; they provide a real roller-coaster ride if they aren't avoided.

Access points are somewhat limited below Troy. Floaters can get out easily at Leonia, Idaho, just across the border, or continue to float all the way to Bonner's Ferry, 20 miles into Idaho.

The Kootenai has a substantial fishery which produces large numbers of rainbow trout and whitefish. Both species of fish grow quickly; three-pound trout are quite common. The Kootenai has earned the reputation of being the best "big fish" fishery in northwestern Montana. Although a good deal of fish habitat has been destroyed to accommodate the railroad, it's still a very productive river. Good insect hatches occur throughout the summer and fall.

In addition to trout, the unusual and rare white sturgeon resides in the Kootenai below the falls. These large fish, which weight more than 100 pounds, should be listed as an endangered species, if indeed they aren't already extinct.

At the turn of the century, old-timers used to think it was great sport to dynamite these big fish at the large pool at the base of the falls. Their method was to float out in the pool on rafts and drop the charges into the water. During one such foray, however,

Happy fish-hooker on the Kootenai. Hank Fischer photo.

a misplaced charge blew up the raft and all the fishermen. Fishing with hook and line—as well as dynamite—is now prohibited for these disappearing behemoths.

Isolated portions of the Kootenai still contain abundant wildlife. The king of all anglers, the osprey, can often be seen diving for fish. Bighorn sheep live on the cliffs near the falls, and whitetails walk most of the thickets. The Kootenai is one of the few rivers in Montana where black bears are commonly sighted; they often prowl along the river in late spring. Bald eagles concentrate along the river in the winter, as do waterfowl.

Most floating pressure on the Kootenai comes from local people, as this neglected corner of the state is far from everywhere. Motorboat use on some parts isn't uncommon.

Trivia buffs will be interested to learn that the lowest point in Montana is where the Kootenai leaves the state near Leonia, Idaho. The elevation is 1,820 feet, substantially lower than most places in eastern Montana.

Once known as Montana's "dream stream," the Corps of Engineers has turned most of the Kootenai River into a nightmare. Until 1972, floaters could cruise for nearly 150 miles through rugged mountains and undisturbed river bottoms on a stream that probably had the most outstanding native cutthroat fishery in the country. Then came Libby Dam, which reduced floating on the Kootenai to a mere 38 miles, and turned the rest of the river into fluctuating, mud-lined Koocanusa Reservoir. It's called "Lake Who-can-use-it" by disgruntled local recreationists.

Sadly, the assaults on the Kootenai haven't subsided. The Corps now wants to build a reregulation dam below the main dam and wipe out another 10 miles of river. As the final blow, an electrical cooperative wants to build a run-of-the-river dam at Kootenai Falls, which would disturb another three miles. Kootenai Falls is one of the few remaining large waterfalls in Montana that hasn't been developed. Disgruntled local conservationists created a classic "Pave the Kootenai" bumper sticker to poke fun at the develop-it-all mentality. Citizens' groups in the Libby area are actively fighting the proposed projects, and they can always use more volunteers and money.

The Madison River

As a kid, I spent an inordinate amount of time in my grandfather's basement, perusing old outdoor magazines. Trout fishing soon became synonymous with Joe and his pal driving out from New Jersey to catch hook-jawed brown trout on Montana's Madison River. The folklore hasn't changed much, and the beautiful Madison is probably Montana's most popular river.

The reasons for the Madison's popularity are well-founded. Formed by pristine sources high in Yellowstone National Park (floating the Madison isn't allowed in the park), the Madison flows gin-clear and undisturbed through lush meadows and broken timber. Large numbers of elk, deer, waterfowl, and other wildlife reside peacefully along its shores, creating a frontier setting. Throw in good access and outstanding fishing, and you have the ingredients for occasional overcrowding.

Outside of Yellowstone Park, two major dams and a natural lake check the flow of the river. First comes Hebgen Dam (only 1 1/2 miles outside of the park), which forms Hebgen Reservoir. Next comes Quake Lake, formed by a major earthquake and subsequent landslide in 1959; it lies about four miles below Hebgen Dam. Finally, there's the Madison Dam, a very small Montana Power project that has operated since about 1900. The Madison Dam, which lies 57 miles downstream from Hebgen Dam, forms Ennis Reservoir and marks the artificial distinction between the upper and lower river.

Floating of the upper Madison starts about four miles downstream from Quake Lake at the State Highway 87 bridge. The short section of river immediately below Quake Lake is extremely dangerous because of fast water and sharp, jagged rocks. The sharp rocks are remnants of the 1959 earthquake, and even experts don't often risk their necks there. It should be good floating a few hundred years from now.

Most of the 35-mile stretch between Quake Lake and Varney Bridge flows swiftly but at a very uniform depth. The river flows in a wide, shallow channel averaging about three or four feet deep, and resembles a long, continuous riffle. Occasional large boulders present the only hazard for floaters. The cannonball-sized rocks that blanket the bottom of the river can cause treacherous footing for waders.

The river winds through some highly scenic country, with the lofty Madison Range to the east and the sage-covered foothills of the Gravelly Mountains to the west. The access is excellent on this upper section, as much of the land bordering the river is

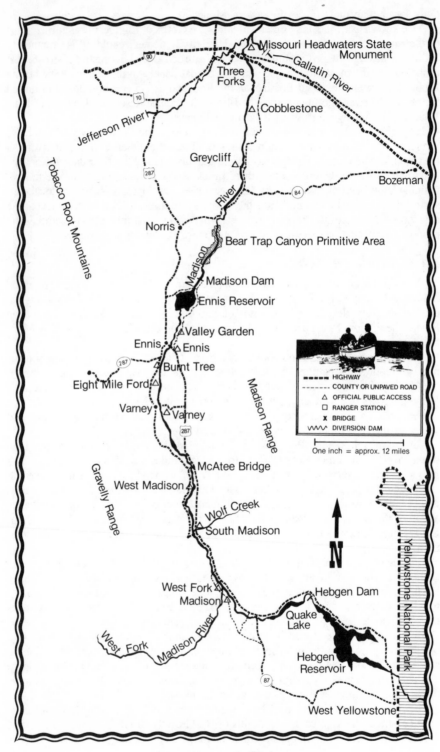

Missouri Headwaters State Monument

Gallatin River

Three Forks

90

10

Cobblestone

Jefferson River

Tobacco Root Mountains

Greycliff

287

River

84

Bozeman

Norris

Bear Trap Canyon Primitive Area

Madison

Madison Dam

Ennis Reservoir

Valley Garden

Ennis

Ennis

Burnt Tree

287

Eight Mile Ford

Madison Range

Varney

Varney

287

McAtee Bridge

West Madison

Gravelly Range

Wolf Creek

South Madison

HIGHWAY
COUNTY OR UNPAVED ROAD
△ OFFICIAL PUBLIC ACCESS
□ RANGER STATION
✕ BRIDGE
〰〰 DIVERSION DAM

One inch = approx. 12 miles

N

West Fork
Madison

Hebgen Dam

Quake Lake

West Fork   Madison River

Hebgen Reservoir

Yellowstone National Park

87

West Yellowstone

Madison River

McKenzie boat on the Madison. Hank Fischer photo.

publicly owned. There are several picnic areas, campgrounds, and fishing-access sites.

As the river approaches Ennis Reservoir, it braids into several channels. Much of the river below Varney Bridge has extensive braiding, and logjams and downed trees will provide obstacles not encountered further upstream. Beginners may want to stay clear. Low summer flows may require floaters to drag their crafts over sandbars.

The section from the bridge at Ennis down to the lake is a good section to see deer, moose, mink, and beaver, as well as raptors and shorebirds. Look carefully for great blue heron rookeries.

Despite the swift current and occasional boulders, beginners can handle most of the upper river when flows are normal—with the possible exception of the stretch between Varney Bridge and Ennis Reservoir. Be sure to watch for low bridges, however. Debris can gather around the pilings and make passage difficult.

Floating pressure on the upper river is extremely high. Recreational studies reveal a 500% increase in angler pressure over the past three decades. The river now supports over 50,000 angler-days annually. Several professional outfitters offer guide service on this section, and it's very popular with tourists and out-of-state anglers. The large number of floaters has created a conflict between float fishermen and bank fishermen. In the past, alternating sections of the upper river have been closed to float fishing. Fishermen are still allowed, however, to use boats to reach fishing sites, but they aren't allowed to fish from the boat. The number of commercial outfitters permitted on the Madison has also been regulated in recent years.

Be sure to check the regulations before making a Madison River fishing trip. In addition to no-float fishing sections, the Madison also has a section closed to fishing and a catch-and-release section.

The lower Madison (below Ennis Reservoir) isn't nearly as popular as the upper section. While this part of the river was once one of the most productive trout streams in Montana, thermal problems have affected the fishery.

Fisheries biologists have learned that during the hot summer months, Ennis Reservoir acts as a giant solar collector, and its water temperature sometimes gets as high

The rugged Bear Trap Canyon. Western Waters photo.

as 85 degrees. Since the lake has filled in with silt and become very shallow, it has no thermocline (the dividing point between warm and cold water). All of the lake gets warm. This water, of course, flows through the spillway and heats up the river downstream.

Since trout do best with cold water temperatures, their growth rates have been dramatically affected below Ennis Dam. In addition, plant and insect life have changed.

While all this is of grave concern to trout fishermen, swimmers and inner-tubers certainly don't mind the warm water temperatures. Consequently, the lower river near Highway 84 (formerly Highway 289) has become very popular with recreationists in the heat of the summer.

Floating on the lower river can begin right below the dam, though not for everyone. Below the dam lies the rugged, inaccessible Bear Trap Canyon, which has some outstanding rapids (see white-water section). The Bureau of Land Management currently manages this nine-mile section of the river (which encompasses 36,700 acres) designated as a wilderness area.

The Bear Trap offers good white-water excitement for experts in large rafts or kayaks. Small rafts or open canoes should stay away. The Bear Trap is doubly dangerous because of its remoteness—help can be far away. Everyone gives dire warnings about the large number of rattlesnakes in the Bear Trap, which reportedly are about knee-deep and attack without provocation. It you see a rattler, don't kill it. They may be all that's protecting this area.

By the time the Madison leaves the Bear Trap Canyon, it's pretty tame. The area near the Highway 84 bridge is quite popular with swimmers and rafters. Once the river leaves the highway, access is rather limited, although Department of Fish, Wildlife and Parks access sites at Greycliff, Cobblestone, and Three Forks occur in about equal intervals in the 18-mile section from the U.S. 84 bridge to the mouth of the Missouri.

The lower sections of the Madison are quite isolated and can have good fishing. One-hundred-foot-high grey cliffs tower over the river, and there's always a spec-

64

tacular view of the Spanish Peaks. Sometimes, the river gets dirty even at non-runoff times, a result of high winds which stir up mud in shallow Ennis Reservoir.

Since fishing is the main attraction on the Madison, it's only fair to tell why. Fisheries biologists, who survey the river regularly, report that some sections of the river contain as many as 4,500 trout over eight inches for every mile of stream. These fish are all wild—not reared in a hatchery—and average about a pound each. The upper river has approximately equal numbers of browns and rainbows; the lower river has more browns. For those who think big, a 7 1/2-pounder that biologists captured, marked, and released a couple of years ago may have grown up by now.

The Madison salmon-fly hatch usually occurs in late June. During this time, incredible numbers of large stoneflies buzz through the air like miniature helicopters, and the fish go wild, as do the anglers, who occur in what seems like even more incredible numbers than the bugs. The river gets so thoroughly flailed that there's foam all the way to Three Forks.

Favorite flies on the Madison include Sofa Pillows and Fluttering Stoneflies during the salmon-fly hatch and old standards like the Goofus Bug, Royal Wulff, and Adams at other times. Big wet flies—Bitch Creeks, Girdle Bugs, and others—can also be productive, particularly early in the season.

The Marias River

Known to the Indians as "the river that scolds at all others," the slow-moving but scenic Marias River is one of Montana's least known float streams. While its headwaters actually originate near Glacier National Park, the river begins about 12 miles south of the town of Cut Bank, where Cut Bank Creek and Two Medicine River join. While floating is possible from this point down to Tiber Reservoir, access is somewhat restricted, and this section is rarely floated. Most floaters go below the reservoir, where fishing is better and the scenery more appealing.

The Marias has a rich historical background. Lewis and Clark camped at the river's mouth, near the present day site of Loma, on June 3, 1805. Captain Lewis named the river Maria's River in honor of his cousin, Miss Maria Wood. Obviously not much of a lady's man, Lewis later apologized in his journal for naming such a silt-laden, unromantic river in honor of his beloved cousin. Historians later dropped the apostrophe from Maria's River, changing the pronunciation and losing a little river lore.

The Corps of Discovery had to make a critical decision when they reached the mouth of the Marias on their travels up the Missouri. Upon reaching this point, the explorers were unsure which branch was the main fork of the Missouri. The Marias most resembled the part of the Missouri the crew had already traversed, as it was slow and muddy. The other fork—which we now recognize as the main fork of the Missouri—was clear above where the Marias entered and seemed to lead to the mountains. Almost all of the crew thought the Marias was the main fork of the Missouri. Lewis and Clark, however, thought differently. After several days of careful thought and evaluation, they made the correct decision.

What if Lewis and Clark had proceeded up the Marias instead of the Missouri? They might have been forced to retrace their path, losing valuable time that could have meant a late, dangerous trip across the mountains in November. On the other hand, they might have found Marias Pass near Glacier Park—the lowest and least formidable path across the Continental Divide.

Lewis and Clark were astonished by the beauty of the rolling prairies that surround the Marias. Captain Lewis wrote, "(the river) passes through a rich fertile and one of the most beatifully picteresque countries that I ever beheld, through the wide ex-

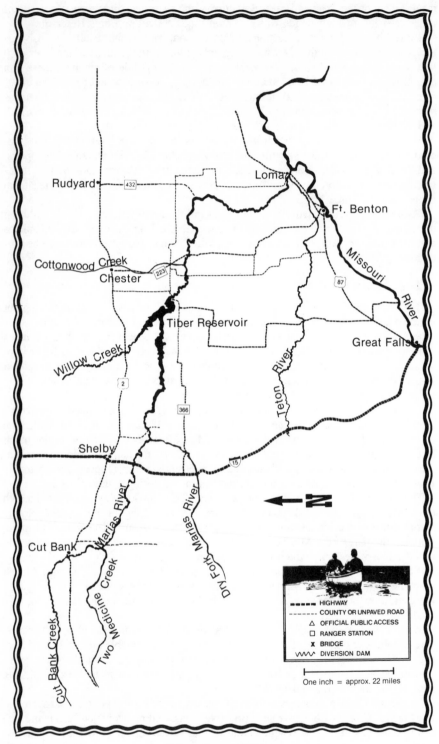

Marias River

Great blue heron. Harry Engels photo.

panse of which innumerable herds of living anamals are seen, it's borders garnished with one continued garden of roses, while it's lofty and open forrests are the habitation of miriads of the feathered tribes who salute the ear of the passing traveler with their wild and simple, yet sweet and cheerfull melody.''

No less ecstatic, Captain Clark reported, "the country in every derection around us was one vast plain in which innumerable herds of Buffalow were seen attended by their shepperds, the wolves; the solatary antelope which now had their young were distributed over it's face; some herds of Elk were also seen; the verdue perfectly cloathed the ground, the weather was pleasant and fair.''

Below Tiber Reservoir, the Marias flows past towering sandstone cliffs and interesting badlands formations. Thick cottonwood groves line parts of the bottomlands. Much of the country resembles the wild section of the Missouri River, only the Marias is smaller and more personal. Like the lower Missouri, the water in the Marias is generally slow-moving and carries some sediment.

The exception to this is the approximately 15-mile section immediately below the dam where the water is clearer and colder than the lower section. A put-and-take rainbow-trout fishery is maintained in this area, and fishing can be good. Access to the river can be found immediately below the dam at a campground. In addition, two county roads and Highway 223 cross the river in the first 15 miles below the dam.

After the Highway 223 bridge, the river remains quite isolated for the rest of its course. One can reach the river via a seldom-used dirt road south of Rudyard, about midway between the Highway 223 bridge and Loma. Ask permission.

Beginners can handle the Marias. Although the dam causes water fluctuations, they

The Marias—a miniature Missouri River. Hank Fischer photo.

usually aren't major. Watch for a couple of small diversion dams and weirs. In extremely dry years, the Marias can get too low to float.

Although you won't see the wildlife Lewis and Clark did (they saw wolves, grizzly, buffalo, and elk) many species still roam the hills and bottoms of the Marias. Both mule and whitetail deer are fairly common. Large numbers of waterfowl typically congregate on the river in the spring and fall. Eagles often winter along the Marias, and coyotes can be seen almost any time. One friend reported he saw over 50 of the much-maligned song dogs in one trip. You'll find, however, that the number of coyotes seen is proportional to the current price of coyote pelts.

Floaters should be aware of the Brinkman Game Preserve, a state wildlife refuge that extends from the Highway 223 bridge east for about six air miles (about 10 river miles); it ends at the Liberty/Hill County line. This little-known refuge, which encompasses nearly 13,000 acres of public and private land, was created by the Fish and Game Commission in 1926. It's poorly marked, and there are very few signs; hunting is not permitted along this section of river except for deer hunting by permit only.

Beavers occasionally can be spotted along the Marias, but they aren't as numerous as they once were. In 1831, James Kipp thought it was such good beaver country that he built Fort Piegan at the mouth of the Marias. He reportedly acquired over 2,400 "plews" in his first 10 days of business, but the trade didn't last and the fort was abandoned.

Warm-water fish such as walleye, sauger, northern pike, catfish, and goldeye inhabit the lower sections of the river, and the experienced worm-dunker can do quite well. Goldeye usually bite on artificials as well as bait.

Summers along the Marias are generally short, but they can be devilishly hot. This area receives extreme temperature fluctuations. Water temperatures in the river can get very warm in the summer. Natural siltation, along with irrigation returns, accounts for the poor water quality found in most of the river. The soil in this area is the famed Missouri River gumbo, rock-hard when dry and stickier than tarpaper when wet.

Because of the impermeability of this soil, small pools of water form when it rains. These provide excellent breeding grounds for a particularly voracious race of mosquitoes. Numerous and quite large, they're sometimes mistaken for small ducks. Take plenty of repellent, long pants, and long sleeves.

The Milk River

Although not a classical beauty, the Milk River contains some of the least explored water in Montana. At first glance, the sluggish and turbid Milk might not seem as appealing as better known rivers like the Blackfoot or Madison. But those who enjoy solitude, wide open spaces, and the opportunity to see wildlife won't be disappointed. The Milk River country is a land of varied landscapes, ranging from rolling hills and badlands to low buttes and shallow valleys. It has a rough, primitive beauty composed of windswept plains once covered by glaciers.

Captain Meriwether Lewis noted the most salient characteristic of this major river while traveling up the Missouri in 1805. He wrote, "The water of this river possesses a peculiar whiteness, being about the colour of a cup of tea with the admixture of a tablespoonfull of milk." Always the astute observer, Lewis named it the Milk River.

While most people think of the Milk as a turbid river, it flows out of the undisturbed slopes of Glacier Park as a clear mountain stream. Then, it enters Canada north of Cut Bank. After a 100-mile loop in Canada, the Milk returns to Montana as a changed stream. The Canadians aren't to blame, however, as most of the siltation is natural. While it was once thought the Milk's bluish-white color resulted from glacial till that

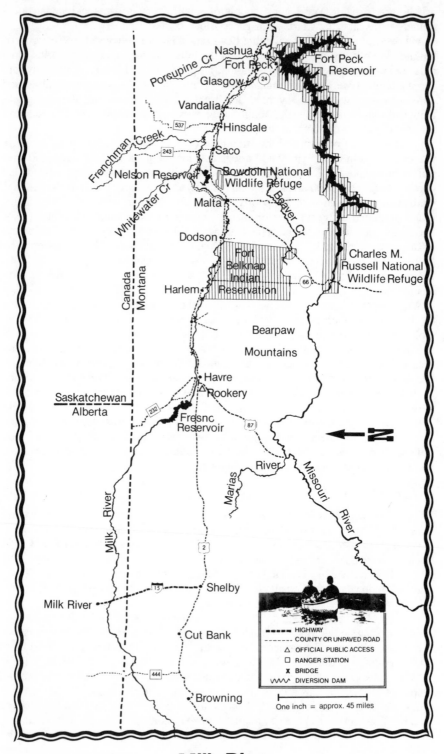

Nashua
Fort Peck
Porcupine Cr
Fort Peck
Reservoir
Glasgow
24
Vandalia
537
Hinsdale
Frenchman Creek
243
Saco
Nelson Reservoir
Bowdoin National
Wildlife Refuge
Whitewater Cr
Malta
Beaver Cr
Dodson
Charles M.
Russell National
Wildlife Refuge
Fort
Belknap
Indian
Reservation
66
Harlem
Bearpaw
Mountains
Canada
Montana
Havre
Rookery
Saskatchewan
Alberta
232
Fresno
Reservoir
87
N
River
Marias
Missouri River
Milk River
2
15
Shelby
Milk River
Cut Bank
444
Browning

HIGHWAY
COUNTY OR UNPAVED ROAD
△ OFFICIAL PUBLIC ACCESS
□ RANGER STATION
✗ BRIDGE
◁◁◁◁ DIVERSION DAM

One inch = approx. 45 miles

Milk River

has accumulated in this area, it's now thought the color originates from fine sand picked up in Alberta in a deep gorge near Writing-on-Stone Park.

The Milk carries a heavy sediment load, particularly in the spring. Some say it's so muddy you can see the deer and raccoon tracks float by; others claim you can walk across it during runoff.

Despite all the jokes about the Milk, it winds through beautiful prairie country that's alive with wildlife. The river occupies a broad floodplain which geologists speculate was created by the Missouri River in pre-glacial times. The Milk doesn't have the rugged breaks of nearby rivers such as the Missouri and Marias. Tall cottonwoods and thick brush often envelop the Milk, creating excellent habitat for deer, beaver, mink, and great blue herons. Sandhill cranes stalk the shallows, and white pelicans reside nearby. Heron and cormorant rookeries can be found along the more isolated sections. The Milk often hosts large concentrations of waterfowl during migration.

Only the ghosts of several once-abundant species now wander the Milk. Lewis and Clark reported seeing buffalo, wolves, and grizzlies, but they all flickered out of existence around the turn of the century, as did the plains elk. The Milk River country was renowned for its thundering buffalo herds and the Blackfeet Indians who hunted them.

Today, along with terrestial wildlife, the Milk sustains at least 42 species of fish, including walleye, sauger, catfish, and northern pike. Limited trout fishing is available a few miles below Fresno Dam.

Fishing accounts for most floating on the Milk, especially in the spring. Anglers often have good luck where tributaries such as Whitewater, Frenchman, and Beaver creeks enter. Probably the most popular section lies between Dodson and Vandalia, which biologists from the Department of Fish, Wildlife and Parks rate among the best walleye stream fishing in the state, frequently producing walleyes over 10 pounds.

The longest Montana tributary to the Missouri, the Milk courses eastward nearly 250 miles before meeting "Old Misery" near Fort Peck. For its last 200 miles, the river parallels both the tracks of the old Great Northern Railroad, the "High Line" Railroad in Montana (often spelled "Hi-Line'), and U.S. Highway 2, formerly called the Theodore Roosevelt Memorial Highway.

Because the river meanders so repeatedly, the actual river distance is probably closer to 500 miles. While the Milk generally parallels U.S. 2, it's usually far enough away that the highway can't be seen or the motors heard. It's an ideal river for floaters who like extended trips, far from civilization.

Floating on the Milk in Montana begins below Fresno Dam and continues to where the Milk meets the Missouri. It's all suitable for beginners. The only hazards on this meandering stream are occasional diversion dams and barbed wire across the stream. Watch for major diversions at Vandalia and Dodson. The Milk can get very high during runoff, which typically peaks in early May. Mosquitoes can be fierce along the Milk in June and July.

Designated access to the Milk is almost non-existent. The Department of Fish, Wildlife and Parks has one excellent site west of Havre (Rookery), and there are public parks at Hinsdale and Malta.

Currently, flows in the Milk River are guaranteed by a 1909 treaty with Canada. Soon, however, the treaty allows Alberta to take its full share of Milk River water. This is a concern not just to floaters, but to ranchers who have more than 120,000 acres of irrigated land along the river.

One option currently under study involves diverting water from the Marias River to the Milk River. Such proposals deserve careful inspection.

The Missouri River

Known as "Old Misery" to the early explorers and fur trappers who fought its tricky currents and fickle moods, the Missouri River has carried several boatloads of Montana history-makers on its waters. Pathway for the expansion of the West, the Missouri provided the major waterway route to the Rocky Mountains from the time of Lewis and Clark until the coming of the railroads in the late 1800s.

Although the river once bustled with activity, it offers solitude and a sense of history to modern-day floaters, and nearly every bend has a story to tell. Despite the problems the pioneers had traveling the Missouri, today's explorers—even beginning floaters—can float its entire distance in Montana.

The Blackfeet, Assiniboine, and Cree Indians ruled the lands along the Missouri before the white man took over. In 1805-06, Lewis and Clark explored the entire Missouri River in Montana and revealed its rich fur resource. Trappers invaded soon after, and the fur trade flourished for several years. Steamships even made the treacherous trip up the Missouri, proceeding as far as Fort Benton. The ships brought gold-seekers, sod-busters, homesteaders, shopkeepers, and other opportunists. The cattlemen took over before the turn of the century and still dominate the area today.

Colorfully named landmarks reflect the rich and romantic history of the Missouri. Places like Gates of the Mountains, Citadel Rock, Hole-in-the-Wall, Slaughter River, Bullwhacker Creek, Drowned Man's Rapids, Steamboat Rock, and Woodhawk Creek all played a role in Montana history. Floaters captivated by lore should be sure to read *The Journals of Lewis and Clark*, edited and interpreted by the eminent western historian, Bernard DeVoto. In addition, check the map appendix for lists of historical maps of the Missouri.

Floods have played a key role in the Missouri River's recent history. As one song describes:

> "She glides along by western plains
> And changes her bed each time it rains."

Pioneers weren't able to deal with the river's wandering ways and set to harness it. Dams now check the Missouri for much of its 2,500-mile flow; in Montana, nearly a third of the Missouri lies locked behind concrete and earth. First comes a large diversion dam at Toston, about 20 miles north of Three Forks. Then come Canyon Ferry Dam, Hauser Dam, and Holter Dam, east of Helena. Next comes a series of five dams near Great Falls that harness the falls where Lewis and Clark made an arduous portage. Finally comes the monstrous Fort Peck Dam in eastern Montana, which drowned nearly a hundred miles of river and created the fourth largest reservoir in the world.

The 149-mile segment of the Missouri between Fort Benton and the Fred Robinson Bridge is the only major portion of the Mighty Mo that has been protected and preserved in a free-flowing and natural state. After a bitterly fought battle, it became a part of the National Wild and Scenic Rivers System in 1976. It's undoubtedly the most popular segment of the Missouri in Montana for floating, attracting river runners from all over the country.

Like a great fallen tree with its branches ensnarled in the mountains, the Missouri starts near Three Forks where the Jefferson, Madison, and Gallatin rivers join. The river flows freely for about 35 miles before being impounded by the Canyon Ferry-Hauser-Holter complex. This section of river has experienced a burst of popularity in recent years, as fishermen have discovered its prodigious supply of trout. Many

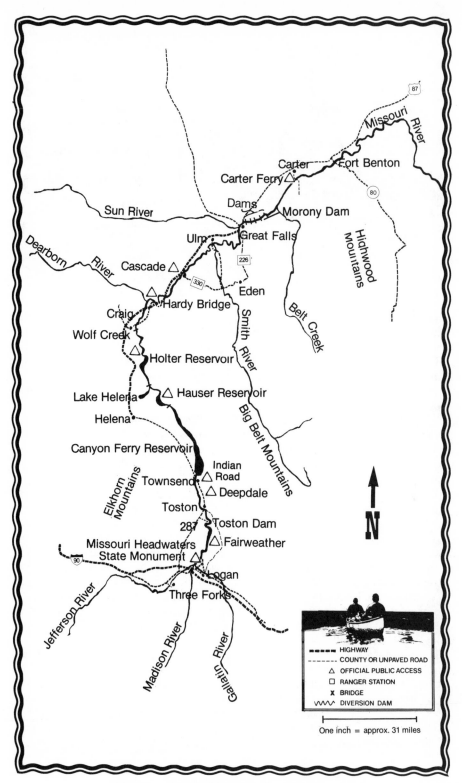

Missouri River (Upper)

Canoeing past Citadel Rock on the wild Missouri. Hank Fischer photo.

anglers name the upper Missouri as one of the top spots in Montana to catch large trout. Most fishermen use big streamers and wet flies to catch both rainbow and brown trout that range from guppy-sized up to 10 pounds.

In addition, this area is fairly isolated and pleasing to the eye as one drifts by rolling hills and wooded islands. Water quality isn't always the best in this section, however, particularly in the summer when temperatures go up. Don't be dismayed by all the rough fish slurping at the surface.

Toston Dam, which lies about halfway between Three Forks and Canyon Ferry, blocks the upstream spawning runs of trout. The Toston-to-Townsend float is very popular in the fall when the brown trout are spawning and the fish are concentrated below the dam. Canyon Ferry Reservoir begins a short distance after the highway bridge at Townsend.

Except for a short float from Hauser Dam to Holter Reservoir, the next floating opportunity is below Holter Dam near Wolf Creek. Here the river flows through a narrow canyon, the same place where Lewis and Clark watched mountain goats and bighorn sheep prance along the cliffs. Although the road is often close to the river, and there's quite a bit of subdivision activity along the shores approaching Great Falls, it's still an enjoyable float. The river is quite clear, and the fishing is often good. For those who want more detail, the Montana Department of Fish, Wildlife and Parks has produced an excellent map of the Missouri River between Holter Lake and Great Falls. The map gives all the access points, plus additional detail; copies are available free from the Montana Department of Fish, Wildlife and Parks, Region 4 Headquarters, Route 4041, Great Falls, MT 59405.

It's easy floating all the way to Great Falls except for some difficult water about a mile and a half below the Hardy Bridge. According to state fisheries studies, this section of the Missouri below Holter Dam ranks with the Beaverhead and Bighorn rivers in terms of producing trophy trout. Studies show this section contains about 1,500 fish nine inches or longer per mile, with about 100 per mile over 18 inches.

The well-known falls of the Missouri preclude floating through Great Falls, but some floaters may want to put in right below Morony Dam and try the short section of white

74

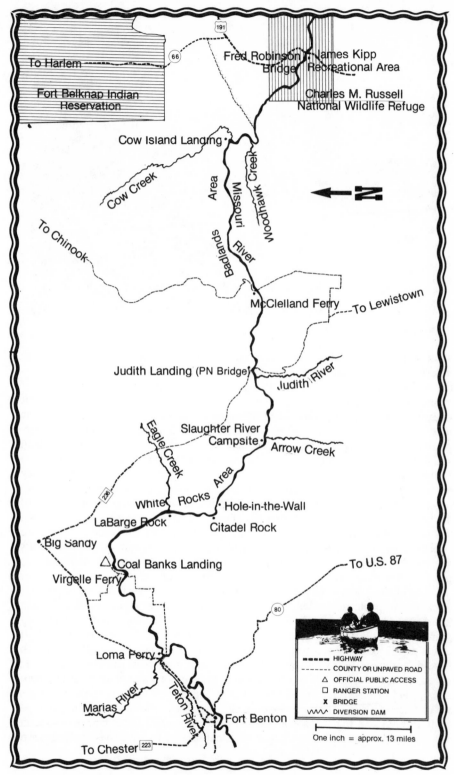

Missouri River (Wild and Scenic)

Hiking in the White Cliffs area. Carol Fischer photo.

water that lasts until about Belt Creek. After Belt Creek, the river is not hazardous
in terms of white water for the rest of its flow across Montana. Although old maps
may show rapids, they're only dangerous if you're piloting a steamboat.

The Missouri begins to change character once it starts to cut into the plains near
Great Falls, picking up sediment and getting more turbid. The Sun River pushes the
first large shot of mud into the Missouri, and the Marias River completes the job.
At runoff times, it justly earns its nickname of "Big Muddy." Some farmers claim
to fill pipes with Missouri River water and then saw them into disks to use as grindstones.

The wild and scenic portion of the river starts at Fort Benton, originally a fur-trading
post. The fort itself is now nearly gone, but the town has an interesting museum.

For about the first 40 miles below Fort Benton, canyon walls slope obliquely toward
the banks as the river slowly sheds itself of civilization. Almost all of the land along
this section is privately owned. After passing Virgelle and Coal Banks Landing, the
river becomes completely isolated as the sloping canyons turn into sheer white cliffs
that rise directly from the river's edge. Wind and rain have shaped the soft rock into
peculiar formations, guaranteed to mesmerize river explorers.

Captain Lewis, always the person for detail, was thoroughly enchanted by this bizarre
but attractive country. His May 31, 1805, description of the white cliffs area is hard
to top: "The hills and river Clifts which we passed today exhibit a most romantic appearance. The bluffs of the river rise to the hight of from 2 to 300 feet and in most
places nearly perpendicular; they are formed of remarkable white sandstone which
is sufficiently soft to give way readily to the impression of water; two or thre thin
horizontal stratas of white freestone, on which the rains or water make no impression,
lie imbeded in these clifts of soft stone near the upper part of them; the earth on the
top of these Clifts is a dark rich loam, which forming a gradly ascending plain extends abruptly to a hight of about 300 feet more. The water in the course of time in
decending from those hills and plains on either side of the river has trickled down

the soft sand clifts and woarn it into a thousand grotesque figures, . . . As we passed on it seemed as if those seens of visionary inchantment would never have an end; for here it is too that nature presents to the view of the traveler vast ranges of walls of tolerable workmanship, so perfect indeed are those walls that I should have thought that nature had attempted here to rival the human art of masonry had I not recollected that she had first began her work.'

After nearly 35 miles of white cliffs, the scenery changes to rugged badlands. This is the legendary Missouri River breaks country, a maze of coulees and ravines that invite exploration. Then, below Cow Island, the valley broadens and the bluffs are lower and more distant. Dense cottonwood stands dominate much of the bottoms, and they're well-used by wildlife. The Fred Robinson Bridge marks the end of the federally protected portion of the river.

The BLM has an excellent map as well as additional information on the wild and scenic portion of the river. These water-resistant maps, which provide a mile-by-mile guide to the river, cost $3. Write to Bureau of Land Management, Lewistown District, Airport Road, Lewistown, MT 59457.

Access points along the 149-mile wild and scenic stretch include Fort Benton, Loma, Coal Banks Landing, Judith Landing (PN Bridge), McClelland Ferry, and the Fred Robinson Bridge. Those looking for only a one-day float usually travel between Fort Benton and Loma. Depending on the speed preferred, the reach between Coal Banks Landing and Judith Landing takes two or three days, as does the section from Judith Landing to the Fred Robinson Bridge. Most people allow five to seven days to float the entire 149 miles. While the widely spaced access points preserve the primitive nature of the river, they make the shuttle difficult. Plan on several hours for the shuttles; hitchhiking is very difficult except on heavy-use weekends.

The wild and scenic portion of the Missouri gets more popular every year, even though other parts of the river are equally appealing. In 1979, the Bureau of Land Management (which manages the river), began a free registration system for floaters traveling between Fort Benton and the Fred Robinson Bridge. Registration is required from the weekend before Memorial Day through the weekend after Labor Day. Permits are available from the river rangers who can be found at Fort Benton, Coal Banks Landing, and Judith Landing access points, or at self-registration boxes at these same access points.

My last "wild" Missouri River trip took place on a Memorial Day weekend, which BLM folks tell me is usually the busiest weekend of the year. Although many floaters were encountered at Coal Banks Landing where I put in (the BLM reported that more than 160 people launched from there that weekend), only a few people were seen during the trip and isolation was nearly complete (read on for the exception).

The number of campsites on public land are limited, however, and the BLM has placed a ceiling of 210 people per day for the section from Coal Banks Landing to Judith Landing, and 234 per day from Judith Landing to the Fred Robinson Bridge. Although visitor use has not yet approached these levels, it certainly will in the forseeable future.

It's now estimated that about 3,000 people per year use the wild and scenic section of the Missouri. Floaters should be prepared for an irritant not usually encountered on a wild and scenic river: motorboats. The droning of motors off the canyon walls not only destroys the naturalness and sense of history that are such a key part of this trip, but they also make the river seem more crowded. The BLM argues that motorboats have a historic right, and that the decision to allow motors was made after extensive public participation. There is a wakeless speed restriction for motorboats, as well

77

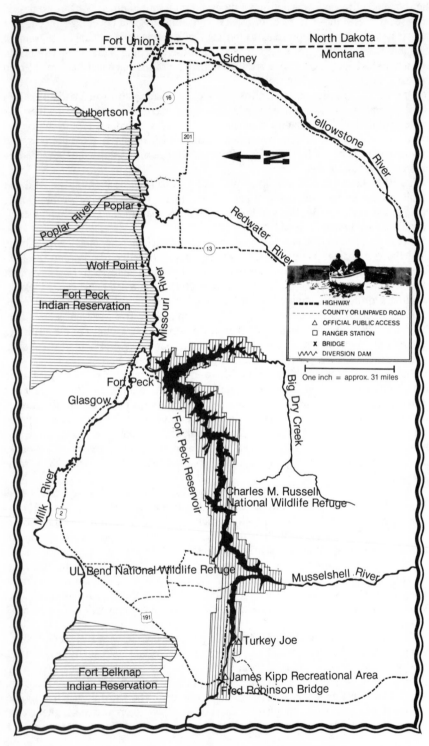

Missouri River (Lower)

Sailing down the Missouri. Carol Fischer photo.

as restrictions against extended upstream travel. Nevertheless, it's my feeling that motorized use on a wild river is both inappropriate and unnecessary, and those who feel similarly should let the BLM know.

Even beginners can handle the Missouri, but watch for a few special hazards; at ferry crossings, low cables can cause problems, as can the ferries themselves, which create an undertow.

Strong winds and sudden storms are common to the Missouri. Stay close to shore if the winds get brisk and stop if they worsen. On the other hand, if the wind is steady and in your favor, use it to your advantage. Try tying a poncho or ground cloth between your canoe paddles for a sail. The person in the bow holds the sail between his legs (to drop or adjust it depending on the wind), while the person in the stern uses another paddle as a rudder. On one Missouri trip, the wind pushed us along so fast we created a wake.

Be sure to take along drinking water, as it's generally unavailable. The river is unsafe to drink unless boiled. When camping overnight, take along gas stoves for cooking, as firewood is often in short supply. Beware of camping in cottonwood groves when winds are strong, as the trees snap easily.

If you're looking for wildlife, head for the prairie-dog towns, as they're usually a center of activity. More than 30 different species of Great Plains wildlife use the dog towns.

Those looking to do a little river-blazing might want to try an early-season trip on the Judith River, which flows into the Missouri not far from the new PN Bridge. In many ways, the Judith is a miniature Missouri, with a willow-fringed riparian zone and a "white rocks" section. The portion of the Judith River that would likely be of the greatest interest to floaters is the section from Danvers Bridge 45 miles to the Anderson Bridge. Be forewarned that this section does have some moderate white water that can cause problems even for intermediates when the river is high.

Expect to see plenty of birdlife along the Missouri, particularly in the spring. Kingbirds perch along the river and grab insects, while many warblers sing from the brush. Pheasants and grouse use the thick vegetation often found on islands, and great blue herons and Canada geese appear along the shores. Look for white pelicans either floating on the river or circling overhead.

Fish in the turbid portions of the Missouri include warm-water species such as catfish, sauger, and northern pike. Night fishing for catfish is a pleasant way to spend a warm summer evening. Others leave a baited hook out overnight and then have fish for breakfast.

Although often overlooked and only rarely floated, the sections of the Missouri River below the Fred Robinson Bridge are also primitive and spectacular. Immediately below the bridge, the river flows for another 20 miles before reaching Fort Peck Reservoir. Bounded on each side by the Charles M. Russell National Wildlife Refuge (CMR), this section of the river has outstanding wildlife values. The focal point is an incredibly productive prairie elk herd, which roams the bottoms and sometimes can be seen swimming the river or grazing on the islands. Deer, turkey, and coyotes are also common.

The prehistoric paddlefish is also a denizen of this section of the Missouri. Spring triggers a spawning run of these strange fish up the Missouri from Fort Peck Reservoir. Fish as heavy as 141 pounds have been taken near the Slippery Ann Wildlife Station on the CMR. Paddlefish, however, aren't taken by conventional fishing methods; they feed on plankton, which are rarely larger than the period at the end of this sentence. Heavily weighted treble hooks are used to snag these fish, which may live 30 years or more.

Much of the land adjoining the Missouri River is publicly owned and managed by the Bureau of Land Management. It's one of the few places one can find true prairie wilderness in the Northern Great Plains. While these lands are currently under study by BLM for possible wilderness recommendation, as yet no real constituency has formed

The Missouri River as it flows through the C.M. Russell National Wildlife Refuge. Hank Fischer photo.

to push for a congressional designation. Rest assured that the time for these lands to receive consideration will probably arrive sometime in the next decade. When it happens, the organization to contact will be the Montana Wilderness Association, Box 635, Helena MT 59601.

Below Fort Peck Reservoir, the Missouri remains primitive. Here, rough breaks country gently merges with woodlands as the river approaches North Dakota. Although U.S. 2 is never far away, this section of the river is quite isolated for its entire 125-mile flow. If you don't like the crowds on the wild and scenic section, this part of the Missouri will please the crustiest of river hermits. In addition, it has a large complement of wildlife. Large numbers of waterfowl use this part of the river which, in turn, attract many birds of prey. Whitetails and geese are common. Fox squirrels, which have recently expanded their range into eastern Montana, can often be seen in the trees near the river. For those really seeking the unusual, this is probably the best spot in Montana to see a whooping crane, as they migrate through this area in the spring and fall.

The section of the Missouri immediately below the Fort Peck Dam is currently threatened by a proposed re-regulation dam. Proposed by the Corps of Engineers and supported by local boosters, it would destroy another 10 miles of the disappearing Missouri, including an important recreational and wildlife area below the dam. Because of its remote location, this project has received little publicity. It deserves more attention.

The Red Rock River

If you're bothered by the large number of floaters on the upper Beaverhead, try driving a little farther south to the Red Rock River. This little-known stream, which empties into Clark Canyon Reservoir, receives only a moderate amount of floating pressure.

In its lower reaches, the Red Rock closely resembles the Beaverhead, both in scenery and fishing. Although it's a little smaller, it turns and twists in the same distinctive fashion and has the same outstanding trout habitat. In its upper reaches, where it flows through Red Rock Lakes National Wildlife Refuge, the river winds through a unique high-altitude marsh that teems with bird life. Much of the 32,000-acre refuge is a designated wilderness area, one of the very few places in Montana where wilderness isn't "on the rocks."

The Red Rock gets its start among the towering peaks of the Centennial Mountains, which lie just west of Yellowstone National Park. In its upper reaches, the river flows through the remote Centennial Valley, one of the most scenic and undeveloped valleys of Montana.

Herds of cattle were driven into the valley in 1876, a hundred years after the Revolutionary War, giving the area its name. The large herds of cattle are still the predominant sign of man. Don't be surprised to see plenty of cows on the wildlife refuge itself. They've been a source of concern for wildlife enthusiasts for many years.

Most people know the Red Rock Lakes National Wildlife Refuge as the place where trumpeter swans were rescued from extinction. In the 1930s, these majestic white birds numbered less than 70, and many ornithologists predicted their demise. Stringent protection brought them back to where they now number close to 1,500 and are expanding their range. These giant birds, which may weigh as much as 35 pounds and have a wing-span of eight feet, have a distinct, low-pitched bugling call that seems to resound across the entire valley.

Floating on the river begins within the refuge on Upper Red Rock Lake. A short paddle across the lake takes canoeists to the river, which snakes its way through a maze of marshy islands before emptying into Lower Red Rock Lake. Since there is

Red Rock River, between the upper and lower lakes on Red Rock Lakes National Wildlife Refuge. Fish and Wildlife Service photo.

little or no current, it's possible to lose your way while picking a path through the marshland. A detailed map of the seven-mile trip between the lakes is available for those who want to take the most direct route. Ask for a copy at the refuge headquarters.

Over 200 species of birds have been sighted on the refuge, and at least 18 species of waterfowl nest there. Shorebirds such as long-billed curlews, avocets, and willets frequent the mud flats bordering the marshes, while gulls, terns, and pelicans wheel overhead. Sandhill cranes are common, particularly in the meadows bordering the upper lake.

Be sure to allow a full day for the trip between the lakes, as it's a slower trip than most and requires a great deal of paddling because of the lack of current. No boats are allowed on this section before September 1 to protect nesting trumpeter swans as well as other wildlife. Be sure to check at the refuge headquarters about boating restrictions.

The float between the refuge boundary and Lima Reservoir, where marsh gradually gives way to open range, is probably the most remote section of the Red Rock River. The river can be reached by a few county roads, but don't plan on hitchhiking back to pick up your car. You could grow a beard while waiting for a ride. About the only time of year people use the river is during the waterfowl season, when hunters pursue the ducks and geese that travel between the refuge and Lima Reservoir. Trumpeters are often seen along this section.

Don't be surprised to find occasional motorboaters on the river between Lima Reservoir and Lower Red Rock Lake; waterfowl hunters occasionally bring motorboats upstream from the lake. You may also be surprised to see occasional motorboats (during the waterfowl hunting season only) on Lower Red Rock Lake, even though it's a

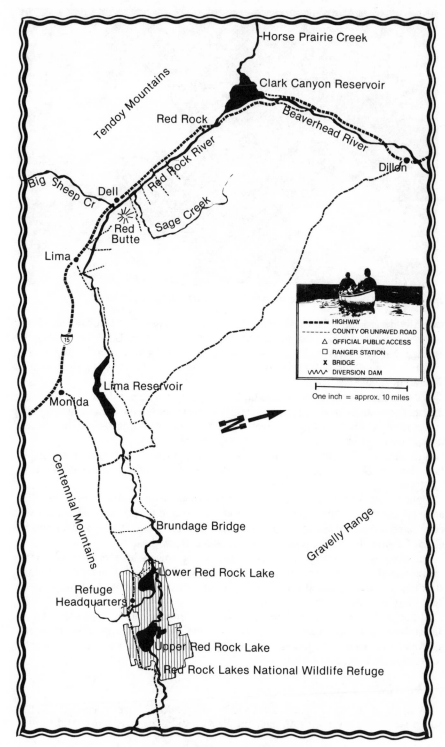

Horse Prairie Creek

Clark Canyon Reservoir

Tendoy Mountains

Red Rock

Beaverhead River

Red Rock River

Dillon

Big Sheep Cr

Dell

Sage Creek

Red Butte

Lima

15

HIGHWAY
COUNTY OR UNPAVED ROAD
△ OFFICIAL PUBLIC ACCESS
☐ RANGER STATION
✕ BRIDGE
〰 DIVERSION DAM

One inch = approx. 10 miles

Lima Reservoir

Monida

N

Centennial Mountains

Brundage Bridge

Gravelly Range

Lower Red Rock Lake

Refuge Headquarters

Upper Red Rock Lake

Red Rock Lakes National Wildlife Refuge

Red Rock River

The trumpeter swan, once near extinction. Harry Engels photo.

federally-designated wilderness area. This exception to the motorized-use prohibition of the wilderness act has been permitted at the discretion of the U.S. Fish and Wildlife Service. Safety concerns during high winds are the alleged reason for this obvious violation of wilderness. If you prefer a wilderness without motors, let the U.S. Fish and Wildlife Service know.

Water quality between the refuge and the reservoir is rather poor, and fishing in this section is an unknown quantity. Reports indicate some trout are present (possible cutthroat as well as grayling), as well as large numbers of ling. All of the water in this section is fairly slow and flat, suitable for beginners.

Bird watchers like the trip between the refuge and reservoir during spring migration. Beware of bad weather, however, as storms are quite unpredictable in this 6,000-foot-high valley.

Floating the Red Rock immediately downstream from Lima Dam is possible, although the river is quite small. It's only recommended for experienced boaters who don't mind occasional portages. The river does get increasingly larger as it approaches Clark Canyon Reservoir, where it becomes the Beaverhead.

The sharp turns, fast currents, and occasional logjams in this section require intermediate skill. It's best floated in a canoe, as the river is a bit small and winding for rafts. Be sure to watch for barbed wire and diversion dams. Low flows in the later summer may preclude floating.

Although this stream is difficult to float, the rewards can be substantial for the determined fisherman. Large brown trout are the quarry, and a good population of the finny monsters can be found in this excellent habitat. Access to the lower reaches is exclusively by country bridges.

The Ruby River

With all its well-developed curves and bends, the Ruby River makes an excellent little sister to the river it flows into, the Beaverhead. The river slinks and turns as

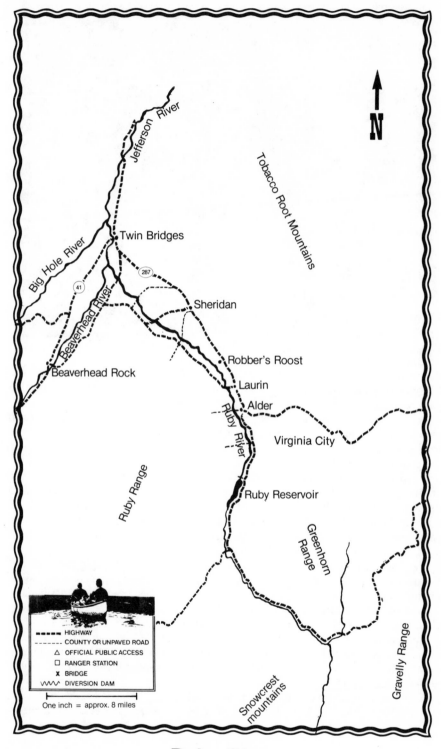

N

Jefferson River

Tobacco Root Mountains

Big Hole River

Twin Bridges

41

287

Beaverhead River

Sheridan

Robber's Roost

Beaverhead Rock

Laurin

Alder

Ruby River

Virginia City

Ruby Range

Ruby Reservoir

Greenhorn Range

Gravelly Range

HIGHWAY
COUNTY OR UNPAVED ROAD
△ OFFICIAL PUBLIC ACCESS
□ RANGER STATION
X BRIDGE
〜〜 DIVERSION DAM

One inch = approx. 8 miles

Snowcrest mountains

Ruby River

Shiras moose, king of the deer family. Harry Engels photo.

it runs through the picturesque Ruby Valley, once the home of outlaws and gold miners. So sinuous is this river that trips involving only a few air miles sometimes take all day. Plan about three river miles for every air mile.

Once the scene of Montana's gold rush, piles of gravel that line the small stream are one of the remnants of the valley's early history. Between Sheridan and Laurin, Robber's Roost, a famous roadhouse for the outlaws and bandits who preyed upon the gold miners, still can be visited.

This small river originates in the Snowcrest Mountains and flows north for about 40 miles before reaching the Ruby Reservoir. After the reservoir, it flows another 25 miles before meeting the Beaverhead. Much of the upper river remains to be explored by floaters. While the river is quite small above the reservoir, it can be floated with small crafts and large amounts of patience. It's primarily for explorers. Almost all of the floating on the Ruby takes place below the reservoir.

The Ruby has been known by a variety of names. The Shoshone Indians called it Passamari, meaning "water of the cottonwood groves." When Lewis and Clark passed through, Captain Lewis named it Philanthropy, in commemoration of what he considered one of Thomas Jefferson's cardinal virtues. (He named the present-day Big Hole River the Wisdom River, also after Jefferson.)

Pioneers later downgraded the name to Stinkingwater River after a large number of buffalo carcasses befouled the water one spring. In more recent times, people have called it the Ruby after the garnets which sharp-eyed people still pick up in the placer gravel of the stream.

While the Ruby is smaller than the Beaverhead, it has the same brushy banks and thick riverbottom habitat. It also has an excellent fishery, and anglers take good numbers of brown trout as well as some cutthroats and rainbows. The thick brush impedes bank fishing, as does the isolated nature of the river. While it's difficult to fish from a boat on the Ruby, a canoe can be useful for reaching otherwise inaccessible areas.

Because of the limited access, small size of the river, and long distances (in hours) between bridges, the Ruby doesn't get much floating pressure. County bridges provide almost all of the access, with most floating taking place between Sheridan and Twin Bridges.

While the Ruby doesn't present any real danger to floaters, it takes considerable skill to negotiate the repeated sharp bends, narrow channels, and protruding trees. Beginners should stay away when the river is high; flows may get too low for floating in July and August. (During the extreme drought in 1985, the Ruby went completely dry in some places.)

While Lewis and Clark termed the river "mild and placid," they didn't encounter present-day Ruby River hazards such as barbed wire and diversion dams. Small canoes (in the 16-foot range) do best on the Ruby. Rafters will have trouble with the bends, and sharp sticks can puncture inflatable rafts.

The river basin has a large number of sloughs and backwaters, making it ideal habitat for ducks and geese as well as shorebirds. Watch for sandhill cranes as well.

The Smith River

Henry David Thoreau once wrote, "He who hears the rippling of rivers will never despair of anything." The bubbling waters of the Smith River have that magical ability to soothe tired souls. Though not yet in the league of India's Ganges River, the Smith is one of Montana's most popular streams, and squadrons of floaters seek a special kind of spiritual salvation along its shores each year.

Located south of Great Falls, the Smith rises out of the Castle Mountains, crooks by White Sulphur Springs, and then courses between the Big Belt and Little Belt Mountains before meeting the Missouri River. Lewis and Clark named the river on July 15, 1805, in honor of Robert Smith, President Jefferson's Secretary of the Navy. The river winds by Fort Logan (first known as Camp Baker), a military outpost established in 1869 to protect ranchers and miners from Indians.

Although the Smith is fairly small in comparison to many Montana rivers, it's a very high-quality stream cast in a near-wilderness setting. The heart of the river, and the highlight of all float trips, is a deep limestone canyon that envelops the river. Long riffles alternate with deep pools on this emerald-colored stream, creating excellent trout habitat. Towering rock formations and thick forests alive with wildlife complete the scene.

With all of these alluring qualities, it's only natural that the Smith gets visited often. During June and July, when the river is usually in top form, pressure can be heavy, particularly on weekends. Those seeking solitude may be disappointed, and good campsites can be limited. Although there currently are no regulations limiting the number of floaters, it's a common discussion topic.

Most floating on the Smith occurs between the Camp Baker access site and the bridge west of Eden, a span of about 60 river miles. Although it's possible to start as high in the drainage as where the two major forks of the river join, only the most devoted river rats try it. Even then, it's usually an early-season proposition, as heavy irrigation use often precludes floating at other times. Only intermediates or better should try the Smith above the Fort Logan Bridge. Beware of a short, rocky canyon not far below the Buckingham Bridge, as it contains some difficult rapids.

At the other end of the river, below Eden Bridge, the river also receives only modest

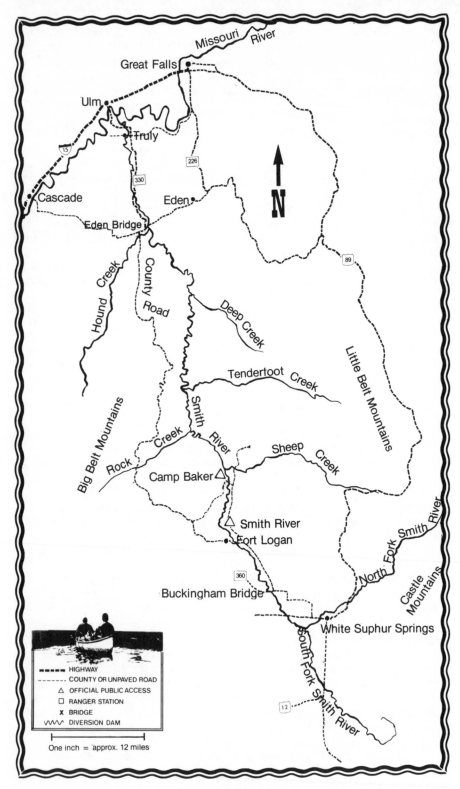

Smith River

pressure. Here it's a flat, lazy river that flows mostly through open farmland before meeting the Missouri about 20 miles downstream from Ulm. Although the scenery isn't spectacular, it can have exceptional fishing for brown trout in the fall, at least as far downstream as the Truly Bridge.

The popular float from Camp Baker to Eden Bridge takes a minimum of three days (plus another day for the shuttle), but many people take longer. The shuttle between these two points is very roundabout so allow yourself several hours each way to complete it. There are two options: the shorter route is a dirt road that's dusty when it's dry and nearly impassable when it's wet. The longer but more comfortable route is via Highway 89 north. This shuttle is hard to hitchhike. Those interested in commercial shuttle service should contact the Great Falls office of the Montana Department of Fish, Wildlife and Parks.

According to a recreational-use study, canoes and rafts are used about equally on the Smith. Rafts provide more stability and are a good choice for beginners and serious fishermen. Canoes are more maneuverable, somewhat faster, and provide a better feeling of being part of the river. Canoes also resist better the headwinds that sometimes sweep up the river.

After leaving Camp Baker, grassy hillsides eventually give way to rocky outcroppings and sheer walls as the river approaches the canyon. By the time floaters reach Tenderfoot Creek, cliffs are rising sharply on each side of the river. Colorful lichens adorn the stone walls, as do swallow's nests and occasional Indian pictographs.

In addition, floaters often spot wildlife. Mule deer are often seen bouncing up the hillsides, and beaver, mink, muskrat, and a bevy of birds (including kingfishers, sandpipers, raptors, and many warblers) are common. I once saw a large mink swimming in the river carrying a muskrat in its mouth. Modern floaters can even count on seeing one animal Lewis and Clark didn't see in Montana—the raccoon. This well-known masked mammal has extended its range into Montana during the past century. Careful

Streamside subdivision threatens the Smith. Hank Fischer photo.

The spectacular Smith River canyon. Hank Fischer photo.

observers may also glimpse river otters and elk, two species associated with isolated areas.

Fishermen sometimes have good luck on the Smith, and the variety of species makes it interesting. Above the canyon, the river supports mainly rainbow trout with some brook trout. In the canyon itself, anglers start to pick up a few brown trout, while below the canyon, browns predominate. Native cutthroats are occasionally caught throughout. (Many fishermen conscientiously release natives.) Fishing is open on the Smith year-round, but there are some special restrictions on length, numbers and species of fish. Be sure to check regulations.

Floaters should also check maps to be sure they camp on public land while on overnight trips. In the canyon area, much of the area on the east side of the river is national forest. Be sure to avoid all private land. Signs mark much of the public land, and the Department of Fish, Wildlife and Parks maintains several public boat camps on the river. Be sure to take water along as the river isn't safe for drinking.

One of the most notable signs of Smith River overuse is the large amount of toilet paper and human feces found behind every likely bush. Keep in mind that about a thousand people per year use this very narrow river corridor, and burying of waste is a necessity. It's gotten to the point where portable toilets are being considered for some of the more heavily used boat camps.

While late spring to mid-summer is usually the prime floating season, those who want to avoid the crowds sometimes go in April (before runoff) or in September, when irrigation ceases and flows come up again. Water levels are usually too low for floating during late July and most of August.

Good places to get information and up-to-date water conditions include the Great Falls office of the Department of Fish, Wildlife and Parks, and the Forest Service's White Sulphur Springs Ranger District. The Department of Fish, Wildlife and Parks has published a detailed Smith River float map, available by writing Montana Department of Fish, Wildlife and Parks, Helena, MT 59620.

One reason for the Smith's popularity is that the floating is fairly easy. Beginning rafters have no problems and strong beginning canoeists can try it, with caution. Novices should stay away during high water or cold weather. Canoeists should avoid overloading their craft with too much equipment or too many people, as an overladen canoe handles like a watersoaked log.

Hazards include frequent rocks (many just under the surface and difficult for the uninitiated to detect), and a few fast runs and sharp turns. In addition, fences may cross the river, as many as 15 in dry years, but usually only two or three. Rafters should be particularly wary of having their crafts punctured by barbed wire and should look for old segments before pulling their raft up on shore. There are also a few cables, marked by signs, that cross the river.

Despite all the Smith's outstanding attributes, every silver lining has a cloud, as those who have floated the Smith have discovered. Upon reaching the heart of the canyon, seemingly miles away from the intrusions of man, floaters round a bend to view a plague of mobile homes and cabins along the river, some so close it appears the occupants could almost dive off the front porch. Subdivisions have sprouted in several areas of the canyon and threaten to compromise the natural values of the river.

Although the Smith is often mentioned as a candidate for the National Wild and Scenic Rivers System, most local landowners oppose this option. On the other hand, some landowners are sympathetic to a cooperative management plan similar to the one established on the Blackfoot River. Such a plan might finally begin to protect the river from inappropriate development, and concerned citizens should follow its progress.

Here are a few Smith River facts (gleaned from a recent Fish, Wildlife and Parks recreational survey) that should provide some good campfire fodder:

- The average Smith River trip lasts for 3 1/2 days, involves 6 people and 2 1/2 crafts.
- 16% of all river floating occurs in May, 53% in June, 30% in July, and 1% in August.
- 40% of the river use occurs on weekends, but every day of the week finds significant numbers of floaters on the river. Here's the breakdown: 21% on Saturday, 19% on Sunday, 9% on Monday, 10% on Tuesday, 10% on Wednesday, 13% on Thursday, and 18% on Friday.
- Most Smith River floaters (40%) are from Lewis and Clark County (Helena)

or Cascade County (Great Falls). Only 1% of the floaters are from Meagher County (the local area where White Sulphur Springs is located) and only 8% are from out-of-state.

• Nearly 50% of all Smith River floaters have floated the river before. This obviously speaks highly of the river's natural values but also indicates a high potential for future overuse if this high return rate continues.

• Fully 80% of the people who float the Smith do *not* think the river is overcrowded. The average floater sees a little more than seven boats and seven people on shore per day.

A final note: Floaters should also keep a special watch for the fabled Smith River hermit. More elusive than a herd of jackalopes and more mysterious than a Montana furbearing trout, he reputedly sports a flowing white beard, a bearskin coat, and always wears hip boots. He spends his winters in a cave, which may account for his legendary nasty disposition. If we're fortunate, he may scare away the subdividers.

The Stillwater River

Mention the Stillwater River and somewhere a kayaker's heart beats a little faster, for the Stillwater is anything but still.

Inappropriately named by an early explorer who must have stumbled onto one of the few quiet spots, this picturesque river dashes madly from the Beartooth Mountains. It cascades quickly through sizeable boulder fields, slowing up only in its lower reaches before meeting the Yellowstone River near Columbus. It's one of the top white-water streams in the state (see white-water section).

While Lewis and Clark never tested the Stillwater's rapids, Captain Lewis camped at the mouth of the river for a week, building two canoes for the trip down the Yellowstone. The dugouts were 28 feet long, 16 or 18 inches deep, about 16 to 24 inches wide, axe-hewn, and hollowed by fire—excellent boats to carry the first white men down the Yellowstone.

Thanks to the 1978 designation of the Absaroka-Beartooth Wilderness, the headwaters of the Stillwater are carefully protected. Kayakers very infrequently float about five miles of the river within the wilderness, but the only access is by foot or horse. The upper river has a distinct alpine flavor, with heavy timber coming to the edge of the river. The entire area surrounding the upper river is very popular with hikers.

Most floaters don't start any higher than the Woodbine Campground, which is at the end of the road. The water is extremely challenging in the uppermost sections—for experts only. The floating season on the Stillwater can be quite short, lasting from about mid-May to early July.

The most difficult part of the Stillwater lies in the three-mile section below Woodbine Campground. The Woodbine Rapids, which start immediately below the campground, last for nearly two miles and are one of the most difficult runs in Montana. At the peak of runoff, they can't be floated, even by expert kayakers.

Just downstream from Woodbine Rapids are Chrome Mine Rapids. Located adjacent to the Mouat Mine, they are also extremely challenging. Both rapids require careful scouting and top-quality equipment, including wet suits, helmets, and high-flotation life jackets.

From Mouat Mine to Cliffswallow fishing access site, the river remains tumultuous, but not quite as dangerous. An annual kayak race (usually the first week in June) between Beehive and Cliffswallow attracts substantial numbers of kayakers each year. It takes about 45 minutes to cover the seven-mile course. The last place finisher gets a bottle of champagne, just for making the effort.

Canoeists won't want to venture much higher on the Stillwater than the Cliffswallow

The Stillwater belies its name. Mike Sample photo.

access. With its broad, gravel bottom and large cottonwood groves, some people compare the Stillwater to western Montana's Bitterroot. The Stillwater has extraordinary water quality for a stream so far east. Like the Bitterroot, the Stillwater can be very difficult during high water, thanks to logjams, downed trees, and occasional boulders. Despite its undeveloped shorelines and good fishing, the Stillwater receives only moderate floating pressure, which is surprising given its proximity to Billings.

Only strong intermediates in canoes should test the lower Stillwater when the water is high. Watch out for a difficult drop about 5 1/2 miles south of Columbus between Swinging Bridge and Whitebird access sites. It gets easier as the high waters recede, but beginners (at least in canoes) should stay away. Watch out for debris that can collect around bridge pilings. The upper Stillwater often gets too low for floating by August.

While the Stillwater now flows relatively clean and pure, it has a cloudy future. Directly adjacent to the main river and the West Fork of the Stillwater lies a mineralized zone known as the Stillwater Complex. This area, which is about 15 miles long and two or three miles wide, contains one of the country's richest supplies of minerals, including copper, chrome, nickel, and platinum.

Because the area holds a great deal of low-grade ore, to date it has been uneconomic

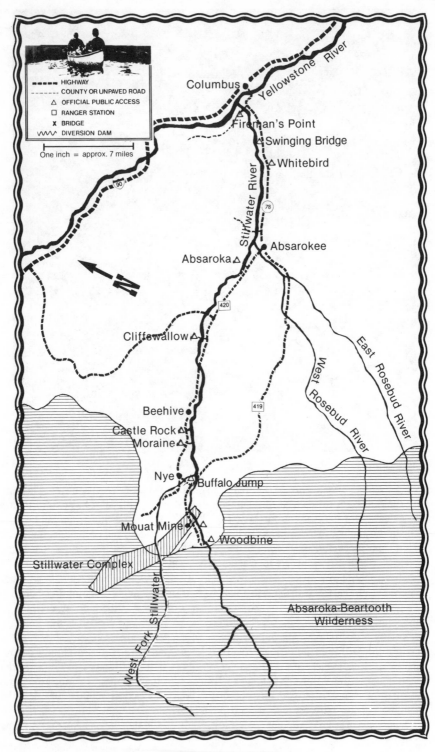

Stillwater River

to mine. The mining industry has been active in this area for more than a century. The companies typically gear up, go into an area, mine like crazy for a few years, and then for various reasons—most of them economic—abandon the area. It's "boom and bust" at its worst.

Right now, the Stillwater is booming again. While the federal Mining Law of 1872 clearly grants the miner his discovery, Montana state law clearly speaks to preserving natural ecosystems. Is it possible to balance a free-flowing, unpolluted stream with mines, mills, and tailing dumps and man's economic needs? The question is difficult, but one thing is certain: if those who care about rivers aren't involved, there won't be any balance.

The Sun River

The Sun River cuts a handsome swath through narrow canyons as it wends its way out of the remote Bob Marshall Wilderness. Early historians often commented on the beauty of this stream as it plunged out of the mountains. The area surrounding the river had special significance to the Blackfeet Indians, who defended it fiercely.

The Blackfeet knew the Sun as the Medicine River, reportedly because of unusual mineral deposits along its banks which possessed remarkable medicinal properties. One can only speculate on how the river came to be known as the Sun. The river flows directly east, causing it to reflect the sun in the morning and evening hours. Viewed from afar, it often appears as a ribbon of light.

What must once have been a bronco of a river has since been tamed and bridled. Gibson Dam, built in 1913, as well as a large diversion dam, now block the flow of the river. Approximately 55 miles of the Sun remain free-flowing, but they, too, have felt the hand of man.

The river remains strikingly beautiful as it leaves the sheer walls of the majestic Rocky Mountain Front. Sawtooth Ridge rises prominently from the south side of the river, and Castle Reef juts just as spectacularly to the north. If the river weren't so tricky, there would be a real temptation to float down backward.

As the Sun emerges from the mountains, it cuts a deep canyon that is unlike any stretch of river in Montana. In fact, it more closely resembles rivers of the southwestern United States, with its towering sandstone formations, multi-colored rocks, occasional waterfalls, and parched surroundings. This section is a geologist's delight as the clearly delineated thrusts, folds, uplifts, and layers of sedimentary rock tell the story of how this land was formed.

Along many parts of the upper river, the bottom of the stream is solid bedrock, nearly as smooth as a pool table. In other places, reefs of rock cross the river, creating ledges and sharp drops. While most of these sections can be negotiated by experienced hands, some ledges drop several feet and may require portage. The rocky riffles alternate with large, extremely deep pools, excellent for swimming. Some of the surrounding cliffs make good diving platforms. The water is deep, emerald-green and usually quite clear.

The canyon section of the Sun starts immediately below the diversion dam (there's an old bridge down a steep dirt road) and continues for about 20 air miles to the U.S. 287 bridge. When water flows are low, it's a long, two-day trip, as the river meanders a great deal. In addition, the constant maneuvering will wear you down. When the waters are high, it's a riproaring trip with a good deal of white water that can be done in six to eight hours.

The narrow canyon which characterizes the upper river eventually gives way to open, agricultural land as the river approaches Fort Shaw. Rolling grass-covered hillsides dominate the landscape, and deer (both mule and whitetail), antelope, and coyotes can often be seen from the river.

About halfway between the Highway 287 bridge and Simms, the cottonwood groves become denser, and the brush thickens, creating better fish habitat than the upper river where vegetation is sparse. Brown-trout fishing can be good where the river isn't seriously dewatered. There's a good deal of wildlife and the river is isolated.

Although civilization remains fairly close after Highway 287, the river bottom is essentially undeveloped except for a few ranches. Almost all of the land along the river is privately owned, and access can be a problem. Most floating access comes via county bridges which occasionally cross the river.

The entire Sun River receives only moderate floating pressure, the most scenic sections lying between Gibson Dam and the town of Sun River. Access is rather limited. The first access point lies on Bureau of Reclamation land about 300 yards above the old bridge, below the diversion dam. From there it's 25 river miles to the next access, the Highway 287 bridge. From Highway 287 to the Fort Shaw fishing access is approximately 34 river miles. Two intermediate bridges cross this stretch; Lowry Bridge, 22 river miles below Highway 287, and then Simms Bridge, another five miles farther downstream.

In all parts of the river, campsites are quite limited and there's very little public land. From the Fort Shaw access to the bridge at Sun River is another seven miles. Below the town of Sun River the water slows and becomes heavily silted at Vaughn with the entry of Muddy Creek. It's not really very scenic after this, as the river more closely resembles a big ditch.

The Sun's difficulty depends largely on its water flows, which can be quite irregular. Although the Sun is a fairly large river, there are many agricultural diversions, and releases from Gibson Dam aren't always optimal. In some years, even the spring flows may be too low for floating. At other times, the river may be bank-full and dangerous. If you're unsure about whether there's enough water to try floating, consult the river gauge on the northwest side of the U.S. 287 bridge near the old bridge abutments. If the gauge reads below 2.00 feet, forget it. At 2.00 feet, it's marginal, but possible if you read water well. Contact the Forest Service's Sun River Ranger District in Augusta for water conditions.

While intermediate canoeists will find the rock gardens and ledges of the upper Sun great fun, these hazards will eat up beginners. Much of the upper river calls for quick maneuvering and good coordination between the bow and stern. Some of the runs must be scouted. When the river is very high, large standing waves can spell trouble for open canoes.

Below the U.S. Highway 287 bridge, the rapids and ledges gradually give way to occasional cottonwood snags and diversion dams. Since this section is quite isolated, beginners should only float with caution at low water. Below Fort Shaw, beginners can try it when the water gets low, but watch for logjams.

While the area surrounding the Sun isn't heavily populated, it has been heavily developed for agriculture. Because of the area's aridity, heavy demands for irrigation water have been placed on the stream. Floaters should be aware of two rock diversion dams between Highway 287 and Simms. First is the Fort Shaw diversion, a little more than three miles above the Lowry Bridge—portage on the left. The other is the Rocky Reef diversion, located four miles below the Simms Bridge—portage on the right. While there are many diversions on the Sun, most don't obstruct floaters. At times, however, they take large gulps of water out of the river, sometimes leaving the river almost completely dry. These erratic flows not only deter floaters, but they also hurt the wildlife

96

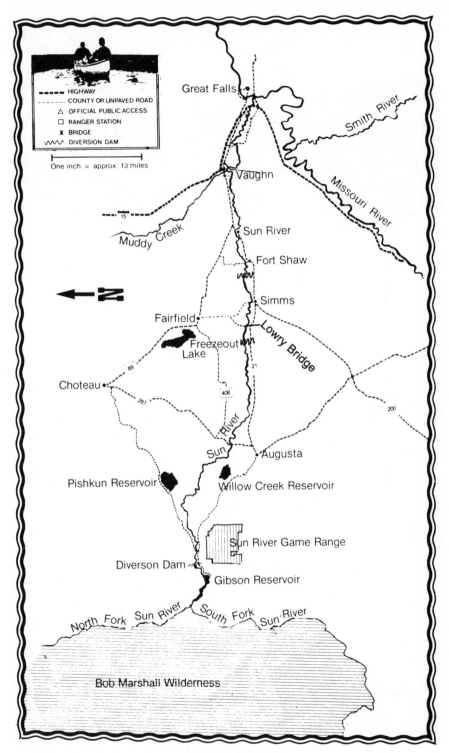

Great Falls

Smith River

Missouri River

Vaughn

15

Muddy Creek

Sun River

Fort Shaw

N

Simms

Fairfield

Lowry Bridge

Freezeout Lake

89

21

Choteau

406

287

200

Sun River

Augusta

Pishkun Reservoir

Willow Creek Reservoir

Sun River Game Range

Diverson Dam

Gibson Reservoir

North Fork Sun River   South Fork Sun River

Bob Marshall Wilderness

Sun River

Upper Sun River. Hank Fischer photo.

associated with the river. The fluctuating flows keep a healthy riparian zone from establishing and hurts aquatic insect populations, to the detriment of species like beaver, mink, waterfowl, and trout. The Sun needs consistent instream flows for fish, wildlife, and recreation. The stream could also benefit from some more restrictive fishing regulations.

The Swan River

Any mountains as spectacular as the Missions would have to spawn a beautiful stream, and the Swan River is that gem.

It arises out of Crystal and Grey Wolf lakes as a cascading torrent of water and then dashes wildly down the mountains until it reaches Lindbergh Lake on the valley floor. From here, it flows more placidly for about 40 miles northward, before entering Swan Lake. From Swan Lake, it meanders slowly for about 10 miles before entering Flathead Lake near Bigfork.

Thick timber and abundant vegetation characterize the Swan Valley, which generally ranges from about four to 16 miles wide. This valley receives more precipitation than most other western Montana valleys—upwards of 25 inches per year. The moisture creates a thick mantle of forest growth that typically comes right to the river banks. Nearly every species of coniferous tree native to Montana can be found close to the Swan River.

Early logging companies occasionally tried to use the river to float logs, but it was too small. In its upper reaches, the Swan is barely large enough to float a canoe, and few people try to start higher than the Condon Forest Service Station. Here, the river has a coarse gravel bottom as it cuts a narrow path through the dense forest.

The abundant trees make a continual contribution to the river; numerous logjams and downed trees are the Swan's trademark. It's difficult and hazardous floating. Consider taking along an axe to make the trip easier for the next floater.

When runoff occurs, trips on the upper Swan can be hair-raising and dangerous. Sharp bends in the river sometimes hide tricky logjams, and the river frequently braids. Don't be surprised to find logs completely blocking the river. Backpaddle while going around sharp turns, and make sure you know how to bring your craft to a quick halt.

About two or three miles above Swan Lake, the river slows down and begins to flow in wide, easy meanders. Beginners can handle this section if they start at the

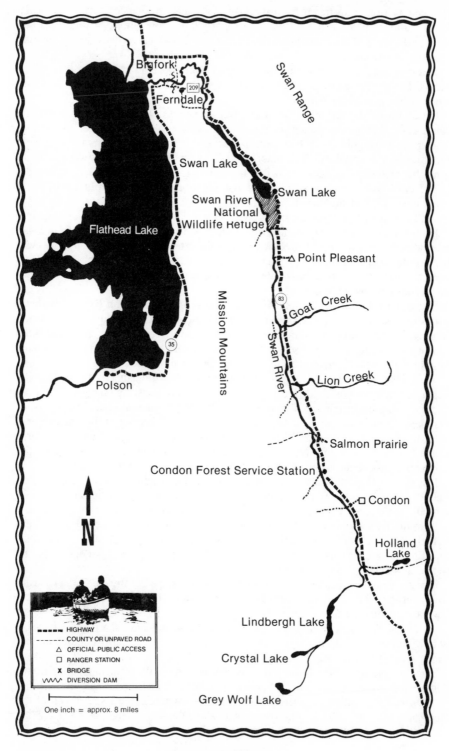

Bigfork

Ferndale
209

Swan Range

Swan Lake

Swan Lake

Swan River
National
Wildlife Refuge

Flathead Lake

△ Point Pleasant

83   Goat   Creek

Mission Mountains

Swan River

Lion Creek

Polson

Salmon Prairie

Condon Forest Service Station

□ Condon

Holland
Lake

N

Lindbergh Lake

Crystal Lake

Grey Wolf Lake

Swan River

first county bridge upstream from the lake. This section includes part of the Swan River National Wildlife Refuge, which supports large populations of waterfowl and shorebirds, as well as deer, mink, and muskrat. This area receives heavy hunting pressure in the fall.

Those floating the last few miles of the upper river above Swan Lake have to paddle across the lake for about a mile to reach a take-out point. Stick close to the shore when strong winds are blowing.

Except for the last few miles, all of the river above Swan Lake requires intermediate canoe skill. Due to the numerous logjams, it's simply not a good river for rafting. The upper Swan gobbles up boats every year, and occasionally claims lives, so note water conditions carefully. Peak runoff usually occurs around the first week in June. Since the area receives heavy snowfall, high flows may continue into July. When the runoff subsides, the river is safer. Spills that might be catastrophic in June will likely mean only wet feet in August.

While most of the upper Swan receives only moderate floating pressure, anglers fish on foot a great deal. The annual run of Dolly Varden trout up the river from Swan Lake attracts many anglers. The Swan provides the extraordinary opportunity for catching a very large trout in a very small stream. In general, however, the Swan River trout fishing is mediocre at best. Special regulations are badly needed to protect cutthroat and rainbow populations.

Except for a few unsightly subdivisions, most of the upper Swan River bottom remains undeveloped and a good place to see wildlife such as whitetail deer and black bear. A few grizzlies prowl the valley, but they're rarely seen. Many species of birds can be seen, though I've never seen a swan, the namesake of the area. Trumpeter swans, largest of the waterfowl, graced the skies in earlier days.

Most Swan River floats take place below Swan Lake. Immediately below the lake lies a two-mile section that's too rough for canoes, but kayakers enjoy it. The float that many Bigfork residents enjoy is a seven-mile trip beginning at the bridge east of Ferndale. From here, the river takes a giant loop, and floaters end this tranquil trip at the bridge west of Ferndale. This is also a popular float-fishing section, particularly in the fall, and one which beginners can handle. If you continue on, watch for the diversion dams about a half-mile below the bridge west of Ferndale.

Just east of Bigfork, only a couple of miles above where the Swan empties into Flathead Lake, lies the Bigfork Dam. Immediately below the dam lies an extremely difficult and dangerous section of water that white-water enthusiasts often challenge.

Here the river plummets 100 feet in one mile, creating an unbroken stretch of extremely difficult water. It's strictly for experts; some avid kayakers run it as many as four times in a day. This stretch is commonly known as "The Mad Mile," and is the site of an annual white-water race.

Floaters should inspect the entire mile on foot before trying this stretch. Rafters usually have a difficult time catching eddies to stop and scout the trickiest parts; even kayakers have a hard time finding resting spots.

As an added danger, many of the rocks along this stretch have sharp edges because of fairly recent blasting. In short, wear a good life jacket, use quality equipment, and be careful.

Since people settled the Swan Valley in the late 1800s, the towering trees have attracted timber cutters. The Forest Service approved the first timber sale in the Swan in 1907, and the cutting hasn't let up much since. Huge clearcuts scar much of the landscape, but ironically, the big trees remain along the scenic Highway 83. They line the road like a Hollywood set, hiding the hatchet job behind.

Tongue River, prairie delight. Hank Fischer photo.

The Tongue River

Probably the most overlooked float stream in Montana, the Tongue River offers easy paddling, excellent fishing, and fine scenery. This prairie stream flows from Wyoming into Montana and provides a unique viewpoint for observing eastern Montana's quiet beauty. The Tongue offers more than 100 miles of high-quality floating before pouring into the Yellowstone River near Miles City.

Scholars sometimes argue about how the Tongue got its name. Some say the river was named after the prominent buttes on the upper sections of the river, which resemble a tongue. Others say the Indians named the meandering river the Tongue because it goes in every direction. Still others say the river derived its name from the Indians who thought it looked like a protruding tongue when viewed from the Bighorn Mountains, the river's birthplace.

Whatever the etymology, floating on the Tongue can start right below the dam that forms the Tongue River Reservoir at the Montana-Wyoming border. The persistent fisherman might pick up a few trout in the first miles below the dam, as rainbows are stocked in the cold tailwaters.

The river winds its way through narrow canyon lands for the first 10 air miles below the dam, and many consider this the most scenic portion. After the canyon, the river flows through lush, cottonwood bottomland, which stands in marked contrast to the semi-arid surroundings. Often visible along the river banks are thick seams of coal, which could eventually seal the fate of this beautiful stream.

An abundance of wildlife congregates along the productive bottoms that surround the river. Whitetail are plentiful, as are ducks and beaver. The biggest turtle I've ever seen in Montana swam under my boat during a Tongue River float. It was easily two feet across.

It was along the Tongue River that an endangered northern swift fox was captured in 1978. These diminutive animals, which are about the size of a house cat, once roamed over much of eastern Montana before they yielded to poison and plow. They were thought to be extinct before this recent sighting.

The Tongue is also a good spot to look for unusual bird life. Double-crested cor-

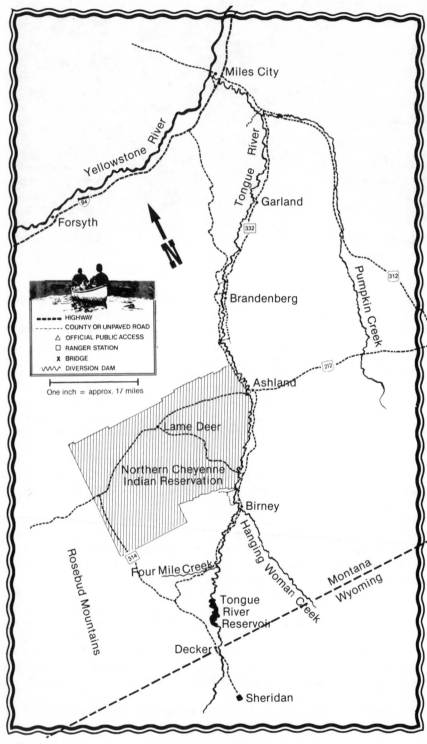

Miles City

Yellowstone River

Tongue River

[94]

Forsyth

Garland

[332]

Pumpkin Creek

[312]

HIGHWAY
COUNTY OR UNPAVED ROAD
△ OFFICIAL PUBLIC ACCESS
□ RANGER STATION
✗ BRIDGE
〰 DIVERSION DAM

One inch = approx. 17 miles

Brandenberg

[212]

Ashland

Lame Deer

Northern Cheyenne
Indian Reservation

Birney

Hanging Woman Creek

Rosebud Mountains

[314]

Four Mile Creek

Tongue
River
Reservoir

Montana
Wyoming

Decker

Sheridan

Tongue River

morants nest along the river, and turkey buzzards often soar in the skies overhead. White pelicans often stop along the river, as do sandhill cranes.

The Tongue River fishery deserves special mention. It claims the title as one of Montana's few smallmouth bass streams and also produces northern pike as large as 15 pounds. Walleyes, sauger, and catfish add to the mixed bag.

Although the Tongue remains turbid much of the year, it usually is clearer in August—at least in the upper reaches. Thick algae growth, however, may make fishing difficult in the summer. The algae usually diminishes after a couple of hard freezes, and fishing reportedly reaches its peak around mid-September. It remains good until freeze-up.

Spring fishermen can sometimes catch the river when it's clear in late April and early May. This period fluctuates along with the rate of runoff, so before leaving home, check river conditions with the Custer National Forest in Billings or Ashland.

In the lower Tongue near Miles City, anglers pursue such oddities as the paddlefish and shovelnose sturgeon, two fish often called "living fossils." Sturgeon in the 15-pound class have been netted by fisheries workers. Paddlefish are known to commonly exceed 100 pounds. A diversion dam 12 miles above Miles City blocks the migration runs of these species.

The Tongue provides easy floating even for beginners. But keep your eyes open for cables, barbed wire, and occasional diversion dams.

Access to the Tongue is extremely limited, with designated access points nearly non-existent. The Department of Fish, Wildlife and Parks plans to purchase some Tongue River access sites in the near future. Meanwhile, be sure to ask permission from landowners before crossing private land.

Because of the massive coal reserves that lie nearby, the Tongue is one of the most endangered rivers in Montana. Major corporations would like to open two new major strip mines near the towns of Ashland and Birney. They would also like to build 80 miles of railroad along the river. Such development could not only threaten water quality, but water quantity as well. Although relatively undeveloped right now, there is a tremendous demand for its water. Developers of irrigations projects, coal gasification and liquefaction plants, and coal slurry pipelines all want to divert parts of the Tongue from its natural channel.

A $32 million dam has been proposed by a California firm that was hired by the State of Montana to determine how to best make water available to industries wanting to develop this coal-rich area. It would be located near Four Mile Creek in Rosebud County.

At the same time, the Montana Department of Natural Resources and Conservation reports that the state-owned Tongue River Dam is in such bad shape that it could collapse during a major flood, endangering the lives of the 500 people who live in the valley below. High water in 1978 did serious damage to the dam, which might cost $60 to $120 million to repair.

The Legislature voted in 1981 to rebuild the dam, but as yet, enough funds haven't been appropriated to do the job.

The Yellowstone River

King of Montana rivers, the Yellowstone flows clean and free for 678 miles, making it the nation's longest free-flowing river outside Alaska. This sinuous ribbon of water, which the Indians knew as the Elk River, originates high in the mountains of Wyoming and flows for about 100 miles through Yellowstone National Park, forming such landmarks as Yellowstone Lake and the Grand Canyon of the Yellowstone. It then flows

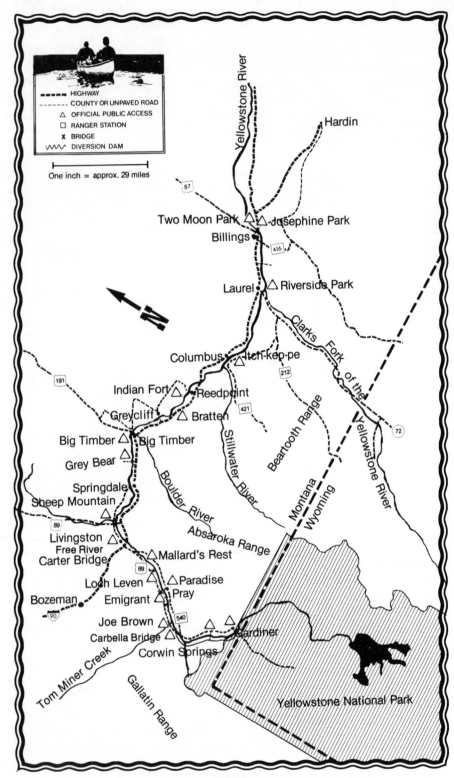

Yellowstone River (Upper)

Paradise Valley, upper Yellowstone River. Mike Sample photo.

across eastern Montana before meeting the Missouri River, just over the Montana-Dakota border.

Few rivers have spawned as rich a history as the Yellowstone. Original pathway to the wilderness, early explorers and fur trappers (including Lewis and Clark, John Colter, Jim Bridger, and Jed Smith), used bull boats, pirogues, and hollowed-out logs to explore the river's most remote points. Later it carried barges and even steamboats, providing passage for miners, cowboys, soldiers, homesteaders, and other pioneers intent on opening the West.

Since floating the river is not permitted within Yellowstone Park, the first place to launch is near Gardiner, where the river leaves the park. This point marks the start of the 103-mile "mountain" section, which extends to Big Timber and is rated a blue-ribbon trout stream.

The upper Yellowstone's fishery is nationally known and needs little introduction. Biologists estimate fish populations as high as 500 fish per 1,000 feet of stream; in the 50-mile stretch between Gardiner and Livingston, this translates to more than

50 tons of trout! Those doubtful of size should visit the "Wall of Fame" in Dan Bailey's Fly Shop in Livingston. It contains the outlines of hundreds of Yellowstone trout over four pounds taken on flies. Conservation-minded fishermen now release most of the large fish which are primarily responsible for reproduction.

The area between Gardiner and Livingston is appropriately known as Paradise Valley. Cold, clear water and cobbled bottoms characterize the river, which flows in long riffles and deep pools. It's shaded by the sawtoothed Absaroka Mountains to the east and the Gallatin Range to the west, which residents claim cast shadows as big as many eastern states. Canada geese nest along the river bottom, golden and bald eagles patrol the skies, and deer haunt the willow thickets and aspen stands.

The Yellowstone's only white water lies in the first 20 miles of river below Gardiner (see white-water section).

Water in the first five or six miles below Gardiner is fast and challenging, suitable for intermediate kayakers or large rafts with experienced hands aboard. Between Corwin Springs and the head of Yankee Jim Canyon, however, the water is relatively flat.

Yankee Jim Canyon deserves special mention for its exciting white water as well as the colorful history behind it. The canyon gets its name from an enterprising pioneer named "Yankee Jim" George, who built a cabin at the mouth of the canyon in 1872 and charged a toll to anyone who wanted to use the narrow road he had built through the canyon. Since this was the main route to Yellowstone Park, the ex-miner had himself a gold mine. Much like St. Peter guarding the pearly gates, Yankee Jim became known as the guardian of Yellowstone, and he was visited by such famous people as Teddy Roosevelt and Rudyard Kipling. Kipling respectfully called the yarn-spinning Yankee Jim "the biggest liar I ever met.'

The canyon starts about 13 miles below Gardiner and lasts only four miles. It contains some difficult white water, manageable by intermediate rafters and kayakers. Canoeists in open boats should stay clear unless they are experts.

Below Tom Miner Bridge, good beginning rafters and canoeists can handle the river the rest of the way to Livingston. Canoeists must carefully skirt high waves, however; they can swamp the unwary. Watch for downed trees and snags as well. Beginners

Canada goose. Harry Engels photo.

should avoid the Yellowstone during high water or cold weather.

Numerous access points contribute to the overwhelming popularity of the upper river. Fortunately, they also help distribute use. Tourists swarm to the upper river during the summer, and many outfitters work the Yellowstone. Expect to see other floaters. Go on weekdays or early in the morning to avoid most people.

The upper river flows north from the park until it reaches Livingston, where it turns east at the point the Lewis and Clark Expedition called "the Great Bend." Livingston lies near the proposed site of the Allenspur Dam which would flood Paradise Valley to form a 31-mile reservoir. Advocates of the dam say it would supply downstream agricultural and industrial users with steady flows of water. The proposal has been soundly rejected by Montana citizens, and the Legislature even passed a resolution opposing it. Now, the Bureau of Reclamation has it on the back burner. Nevertheless, it still looms as a major threat to the upper river.

Between Livingston and Big Timber, the fishing remains excellent, and floating pressure lessens. Floating gets a little more hazardous, however, as the river begins to braid and there can be tricky currents where the channels rejoin. Side channels may be blocked with trees, so stick to the main channel. Beginners can handle this section if they stay alert.

Between Big Timber and the confluence with the Bighorn River (near Custer), is the 160-mile "transition" section of the Yellowstone. Here the river changes from a mountain stream to a prairie river, and the water gets warmer. The river valley opens up as yellowish bluffs (the river's namesake) and rocky outcroppings flank the stream. On one such outcropping, one can find "William Clark, 1806," scrawled on the rock. Clark named the formation Pompey's Pillar, in honor of the infant son of the party's guide, Sacajawea.

Much of this section runs in a braided channel, as free-flowing rivers typically do. Peak flows in the spring create islands, bars, backwaters, and the kind of riparian diversity that makes ideal wildlife habitat. Indeed, this is still the excellent beaver country which early fur trappers told tall tales about. Other furbearers such as mink, muskrat, and otter (only a few), lurk in the cottonwood-willow bottoms that border the river. Geese and ducks raise their young on the islands, and great blue heron rookeries can be found in those areas where few people travel. Whistling swans and sandhill cranes use the river heavily during migration.

It was along this section of the Yellowstone that Captain Clark was struck silent by incredible numbers of wildlife which the Corps of Discovery observed. He finally wrote in his journal, on July 24, 1806: ". . . for me to mention or give an estimate of the differant Species of wild animals on this particularly Buffalow, Elk Antelopes & Wolves would be increditable. I shall therefore be silent on the subject further. So it is we have a great abundance of the best of meat."

Although the trout fishing is not quite as good below Big Timber, the scenery is still superb. Department of Fish, Wildlife and Parks access points provide most of the river entry. Although Interstate 90 and Interstate 94 parallel the Yellowstone for its entire run across eastern Montana, they're usually unnoticeable.

Each July, a Livingston-to-Billings float trip attracts hundreds of participants, many of whom give a literal twist to the notion of getting "Yellowstoned." Beginners can handle this section if they are cautious and don't drink too much. Watch for weirs and diversions.

The "prairie" section of the Yellowstone flows for about 300 miles below the mouth of the Bighorn River before reaching North Dakota and the Missouri River. This section is one of Montana's great untapped recreational resources. Winding through wooded

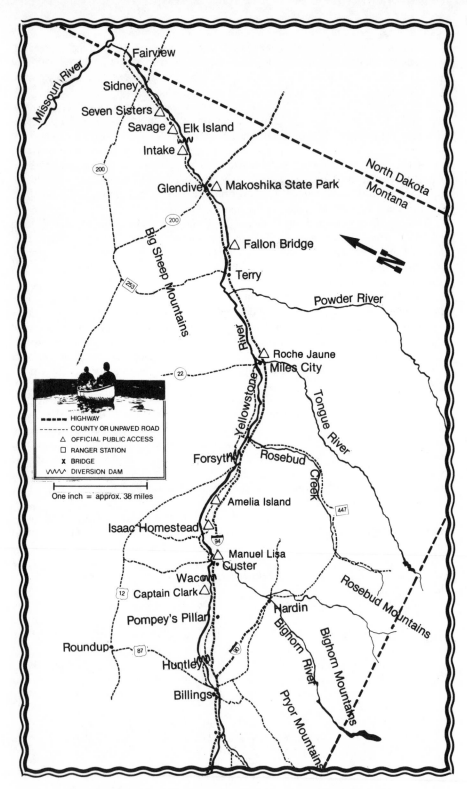

Yellowstone River (Lower)

The lower Yellowstone near Sidney, with coal seams visible in the yellowish bluffs. Bill Schneider photo.

bottom lands shaded by rocky bluffs, a lower Yellowstone trip offers solitude and easy floating. The only real hazards are occasional weirs and diversions. The four most dangerous diversions are at Huntley, Waco, Forsyth, and Intake. Be prepared for difficult, unmarked portages at Forsyth and Intake; there are channels around the diversions at Huntley and Waco, but no signs marking them.

Anyone considering a lower-Yellowstone River float trip should be aware of an outstanding publication of the Montana Department of Fish, Wildlife and Parks entitled "Treasure of Gold." This float guide, which covers the Yellowstone from Billings to the Missouri confluence, provides in-depth information on history, geology, and biology as well as detailed information about access points and hazards. It's available for $1 by writing the Montana Department of Fish, Wildlife and Parks, Helena, MT 59620. It's also available from regional offices in Billings and Miles City.

Despite the aridity of the country it flows through, the prairie section of the Yellowstone contains a greater diversity and abundance of wildlife than any other part of the river. The river itself supports at least 45 species of fish, including two ancient rarities (the paddlefish and the shovelnosed sturgeon) and a freshwater cod (the burbot or ling). Walleyes, sauger, northern pike, and channel catfish add to the fisherman's smorgasbord. Fishing can be quite good, particularly where tributaries enter the river.

The lower river often sustains some unexpected avian species, including white pelicans, eared grebes, and double-crested cormorants. The endangered whooping cranes occasionally visit the river during migration, and sandhill cranes and whistling swans are common. Antelope can often be seen from the river.

Although a few organized float trips are conducted each year between Forsyth and Miles City, the lower river is usually devoid of people. While access isn't as good as on the upper river, highway bridges and occasional Department of Fish, Wildlife and Parks access sites suffice. Beginners can handle the lower river except during runoff. It's ideal for an extended boat trip.

The most serious threat to the Yellowstone is clearly visible along the banks of the lower river—thick, black-banded layers of coal. Captain Clark observed these "straters" of coal, as did an 1876 journalist by the name of Finerty. He predicted, "Someday, I think, when the Sioux are all in the happy hunting ground, this valley will rival the

Lehigh of Pennsylvania." Industrial forces who want the Yellowstone's limited water have tried their best to make Finerty's woeful forecast come true.

They met a strong setback in 1978 when the Montana Board of Natural Resources and Conservation announced that substantial amounts of water will remain in the Yellowstone for the benefit of fish and wildlife and water quality. Unless legal challenges or the Montana Legislature change this decision, it will mean that Montana has turned away from the path of massive industrial development and toward preservation of the natural values of the river while maintaining present uses, which are primarily agricultural. If trout could cheer or beavers could applaud, their clamor might be heard for the length of the river.

The Yellowstone River has consistently been mentioned as a prime candidate for the National Wild and Scenic Rivers System. Such designation would protect the river from inappropriate development such as Allenspur Dam or shoreline subdivisions. Those who would like to help write the final chapter on the Yellowstone River should stay alerted for developments in the long battle to keep the river free.

Montana's white water

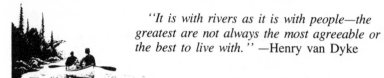

"It is with rivers as it is with people—the greatest are not always the most agreeable or the best to live with." —Henry van Dyke

Should you overhear a Montanan talking about "haystacks" and "roostertails," don't automatically assume he's talking about his home on the range. These words are part of the vocabulary of Montana's sizeable corps of white-water enthusiasts.

Although most Montana white water lends itself to one-day trips, many of the prime white-water runs are extremely challenging. While huge waves and tremendous water volumes can be found on big rivers like the Clark Fork and the Flathead, small rivers like the West Gallatin and the Stillwater offer intense technical rapids amidst gardens of rocks.

This is by no means a complete guide to Montana white water; there are many short white-water stretches and many small streams that may provide excitement during spring runoff that I haven't mentioned. I've only tried to cover the primary white-water spots in this special section. There's good white water on the Yaak River, on Rock Creek, on Belt Creek, on the Judith River and on many other rivers.

For this special white-water section, I have used the International Scale for Grading River Difficulty to help boaters compare different runs on different rivers. See the chart for an interpretation of this system. Bear in mind, of course, that changes in water levels can dramatically change the ratings, so use them only as a general guide.

Blackfoot River

Over the past decade western Montana's Blackfoot River has earned the reputation of being one of Montana's top white-water canoe streams, particularly in May and June during high water. The Blackfoot is a glacial stream, studded with rocks, that occasionally gets squeezed into short canyons. The result is a dashingly beautiful stream that's capable of providing outstanding white-water excitement.

Few white-water enthusiasts start much higher on the Blackfoot than the County Line fishing access site. While there are some frisky waves and a few rapids above this point, they tend to be fairly far apart.

The white water starts not far below the County Line access point, and some of the toughest rapids occur about three miles from the access point, near the old Bear Creek bridge pilings. Between this point and the Clearwater Bridge are a couple of drops with big rocks and high waves. Most of the drops are followed by big pools, allowing time for recovery if problems occur. In high water, only strong intermediate canoeists or better should try this section; without air bags there's the constant danger of being swamped. At high flows, the section from the County Line access to the

International Scale for Grading River Difficulty

Rating White Water	River or Individual Rapids Characteristics	Skills Needed
I	EASY—Sand banks, bends without difficulty, occasional small rapids with waves regular and low. Correct course easy to find, but care needed with minor obstacles such as pebble banks, fallen trees, etc., especially on narrow rivers. River speed less than hard back-paddling speed.	PRACTICED BEGINNER
II	MEDIUM—Fairly frequent but unobstructed rapids, usually with regular waves, easy eddies, and easy bends. Course generally easy to recognize. River speeds occasionally exceeding hard back-paddling speed.	INTERMEDIATE
III	DIFFICULT—Maneuvering in rapids necessary. Small falls, large regular waves covering boat, numerous rapids. Main current may swing under bushes, branches or overhangs. Course not always easily recognizable. Current speed usually less than fast forward paddling speed.	EXPERIENCED
IV	VERY DIFFICULT—Long, rocky rapids with difficult and completely irregular broken water which must be run head on. Very fast eddies, abrupt bends and vigorous cross currents. Difficult landings increase hazard. Frequent inspections necessary. Extensive experience necessary.	HIGHLY SKILLED (Several years experience with original group)
V	EXCEEDINGLY DIFFICULT—Either very long or very mean waves, usually wild turbulence capable of picking up a boat and boater and throwing them several feet. Extreme congestion in cross current. Scouting difficult from shore and some danger to life in the event of a mishap.	TEAM OF EXPERTS
VI	LIMIT OF NAVIGABILITY—All previously mentioned difficulties increased to the limit. Only negotiable at favorable water levels. Cannot be attempted without risk of life.	TEAM OF EXPERTS (Taking precaution)

Roundup Bar bridge is mostly Class II water with a few places Class III; at lower flows, it's all Class I or II water.

After the Clearwater Bridge there's a respite for a couple of miles before reaching more difficult white water about a mile above the Roundup Bar Bridge. The easy access to the big rock garden immediately above the bridge makes this a popular spot with kayakers. The white water continues for several miles below the Roundup Bar Bridge, with plenty of big rocks presenting challenging obstacles. In high water, the rapids here can be fairly continuous, allowing little time for recovery if there's an upset.

The quiet water lasts from Nine Mile Prairie to Whitaker Bridge, a distance of about six river miles. Not far after Whitaker Bridge comes the Blackfoot's most famous piece of white water—Thibideau Rapids. Like most Blackfoot rapids, there's a good drop and lots of rocks. There are several other good rapids in the next few miles below Whitaker before the usual takeout point, Johnsrud Park. Again, most of the river between the Roundup Bar Bridge and Johnsrud is either Class I or II except during high water when the larger drops become Class III.

When the river is high, even the 10-mile section between Johnsrud Park and the weigh station at Bonner can be exciting. It's all Class II or less water, but high waves develop and the current is very fast. This section is the scene of an annual white-water canoe race, usually held around Memorial Day weekend.

While the Blackfoot doesn't have the huge white water of an Alberton Gorge or Bear Trap Canyon, it can be quite challenging and very dangerous in the spring when flows are high and the water is cold. Because of the dangers associated with cold water in the spring, only strong intermediate rafters or better should try the river at this time. Wetsuits, ropes, and throw bags—as well as some dry clothes and matches—are standard gear. Keep in mind the 100-degree rule: if the air temperature and water temperature combined do not exceed 100 degrees, there's a real danger of hypothermia. It's a smart policy to go with several boats to a party. Always be sure one or more persons with each boat is experienced and knows the river.

Once the water drops, which is usually by mid-July, less experienced rafters and canoeists can try their luck. While parts of the Blackfoot can be floated by beginning rafters, it will still take intermediate canoeists to avoid the rocks. It's a great river for canoeists with experience on rivers like the Clark Fork and Bitterroot to try and get better. Be prepared for a possible upset, however, and have your gear lashed securely.

For information on Blackfoot River water levels, call the Trail Head in Missoula at 543-6966. If you're looking for an outfitted trip on the Blackfoot, a good bet is Water Ouzel River Trips out of Missoula at 728-7545. A low-budget alternative would be to check the University of Montana's Outdoor Recreation Program (243-5072) to see when they have trips scheduled.

Clark Fork River

When anyone talks about white water on the Clark Fork, you can be sure they're talking about Alberton Gorge, also known as Cyr Canyon or the Fish Creek Gorge. Bolstered by the influx of both the Bitterroot and Blackfoot rivers, the Clark Fork is a large river when it enters the gorge (the Clark Fork is the largest river in the state as it exits Montana). This 20-mile white-water section, which begins just west of Alberton, has some outstanding rapids in a very beautiful, isolated setting. Although Interstate 90 parallels the river for the entire section, it's only noticeable in the three places where bridges span the river. For the most part, the gorge provides a semi-

Rest Stop Rapids in Alberton Gorge on the Clark Fork River. Western Waters photo by Mark Gibbons.

wilderness experience, with very little development or other signs of human use.

Access to the gorge is rather limited. The standard Alberton Gorge all-day trip starts at the Cyr access and ends up at the Forest Grove access. Most of the white-water action comes in the first part of the trip; after Fish Creek, there's very little difficult water.

Those starting at Cyr will miss one of the best early season white-water spots, the Rest Stop Rapids located next to the rest stop on Interstate 90. If you want to hit the Rest Stop Rapids, put in at the St. Johns Fishing Access Site. Be forewarned, however, that the rapids are immediately below the put-in, so there's little time to get acclimated to the river before the white-water action starts. An alternative would be to put in at the Petty Creek access to get used to the river before hitting this formidable spot. In high water, the Rest Stop Rapids can be extremely difficult—experts only—with big waves and a huge hole; it's a Class IV rapid at peak flows. When the water is low, it's a routine Class II.

For the first couple miles after the Cyr access there are only minor rapids (Class II) before coming to a tough spot known as the Shelf Rapids or the Cliffside Rapids. As one name implies, it's easily recognized by the sharp cliffs. This section not only has some big waves, but there are some jagged sleeper rocks that leave only a narrow passage through a slot in a rock shelf that crosses the river. It's a solid Class III run. There are a couple more good rapids (Class III in high water, Class II otherwise) before the river rushes under the spot identified by three bridges spanning the river in close proximity.

The most difficult rapids in the gorge come only a short distance after the triple bridges. The canyon narrows significantly in this two-mile section of river, and at high flows the rapids are continuous and the current is incredibly swift. The gorge's most difficult rapid, Tumbleweed, lies in this section. It's easy to know when you're getting close, as the river gets very narrow. There's a huge rock on the right side of the river (it's submerged at high water) with a big hole behind. Be sure to scout Tumbleweed (pull out on the left) before going through if you're unfamiliar with it. At low flows it's a Class III rapid, but at high flows it's a very difficult Class IV. A flip at high water can mean a long and dangerous swim.

Immediately downstream from Tumbleweed come two more of the gorge's toughest

114

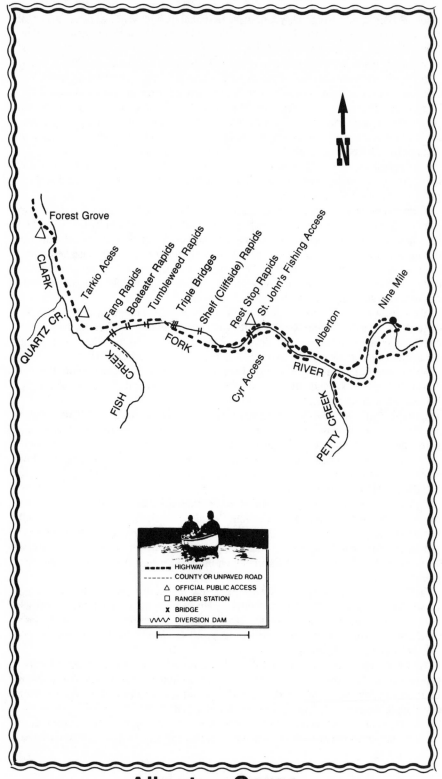

Forest Grove

CLARK

QUARTZ CR.

Tarkio Acess

FISH CREEK

Fang Rapids

Boateater Rapids

Tumbleweed Rapids

FORK

Triple Bridges

Shelf (Cliffside) Rapids

Cyr Access

Rest Stop Rapids

St. John's Fishing Access

RIVER

Alberton

Nine Mile

PETTY CREEK

HIGHWAY
COUNTY OR UNPAVED ROAD
△ OFFICIAL PUBLIC ACCESS
☐ RANGER STATION
✗ BRIDGE
〰〰 DIVERSION DAM

Alberton Gorge

rapids: Boateater and Fang. They both have tremendous high waves at peak flows that are capable of flipping even large boats. While not technically difficult, they are strong Class III rapids at high flows and Class II at low water. After Fang it's only a short run to where Fish Creek enters the river; from Fish Creek on, it's Class I and II water.

There are two standard takeout points for gorge trips: Tarkio and Forest Grove. The Tarkio access is currently privately owned, although the Montana Department of Fish, Wildlife and Parks is negotiating with the landowner for purchase. In the past, the landowner has kept the access open as long as people don't litter. The poorly maintained road to the river comes down a steep hill, and people frequently get stuck at the bottom. The best advice is to leave your car at the top.

The alternative is to float on down to Forest Grove, another five miles downriver, where there's a good developed access that's publicly owned. There's outstanding scenery and good fishing between Tarkio and Forest Grove.

While it's not recommended for standard access, there's an emergency takeout where Fish Creek enters the gorge. It's a steep, narrow trail generally used by kayakers. The site where Fish Creek enters is a favorite stopping point for boaters, and the area is starting to show the signs of heavy use. A portable toilet was finally installed at the creek because of sanitation problems. There have also been problems with early-season floaters building big fires at the creek mouth. Please be mindful of these problems and consider stopping for lunch at some other point.

Like almost any river, the character of the gorge changes dramatically based on the water flows. Places like the Rest Stop Rapids become extremely formidable in high water, while other normally difficult rapids may wash out. On the other hand, some rapids come into their own at lower flows, becoming more technical.

Good white water can be found anywhere between 2,000 and 10,000 cubic feet per second. Between 10,000 and 20,000 cfs, the river gets much more difficult and dangerous. (Normal peak flow generally is between 18,000 and 22,000 cfs.) Above 20,000 cfs, the currents and high waves get extremely treacherous, and at maximum flows—which may approach 40,000 cfs—the flows are so fast and the water so turbulent that a long swim—perhaps a half-mile or longer—is likely if your boat flips. Given the extremely cold water temperatures, it can make for very dangerous conditions. Best bet for flow information is the University of Montana Outdoor Resource Center (243-5072) or the Trail Head in Missoula (543-6966).

High water and cold temperatures that accompany it make the gorge safe only for advanced intermediates and experts at high flows. Be sure to have more than one raft in your party in case of trouble. High-quality life jackets—vest-style rather than the inadequate horse-collar type—are a necessity. Big rafts with rowing frames (14-foot and up with 20-inch tubes) are the standard equipment for runs from mid-May through June.

The gorge has some very large waves and a few rapids that can be life-threatening at peak flows. In a normal year, paddle rafts are a possibility after early July and smaller boats get to be more fun as the water drops further. When the water is really low, you'll even see some thrill-seekers trying the gorge in canoes, but this is only for experts who don't mind getting wet.

The river sees its peak use in late July and August, when summertime temperatures send people to the river for respite. Be wary of combining too much alcohol with an Alberton Gorge trip, as the rapids are difficult and it's not unusual to flip a raft or have people thrown out. Life jackets are an absolute must.

Unless you are a very experienced boater, don't try the gorge at high water unless you're going with someone who knows the river and can handle it. At any water level, every boat should have at least one experienced leader who can take over if there's trouble.

If you don't have friends with experience, there are at least two alternatives. Several outfitters take people down the gorge, the most experienced being Water Ouzel Whitewater Trips (728-7545) and Western Waters (728-6161), both in Missoula. Another choice would be to check with the University of Montana's Outdoor Recreation Program (243-5072) to see when they have trips scheduled.

Flathead River

While most of the mainstem Flathead River flows calm and flat, the six-mile section of river located just below Kerr Dam, south of Polson, is a definite exception. Known commonly as Buffalo Rapids, its aquamarine waters offer big-river white water in a very scenic setting.

The standard starting point for a Buffalo Rapids trip is immediately below Kerr Dam. Keep in mind that this section of river lies completely within the Flathead Indian Reservation, and tribal permits are necessary for use of the river. While public access is permitted at the Kerr Dam put-in site, it is privately owned.

A complicating factor involving Buffalo Rapids white-water trips are the fluctuating water levels from Kerr Dam. While the average summertime flows are about 10,000 to 13,000 cubic feet per second, they commonly get as low as 2,000 cfs or as high as 25,000 cfs. During spring runoff, peak flows can reach 50,000 cfs.

Surprisingly enough, the most difficult conditions do not occur at peak flows; in fact, when the river gets over 20,000 cfs many of the rapids wash out, and over 30,000 cfs, most of the big waves disappear and are replaced by wicked currents and whirlpools. A flip at peak flows, even with a life jacket, can be a dangerous experience. Bear in mind this is an extremely large river with huge flows, making the water extraordinarily powerful. It's sheer folly not to wear a life jacket. The best white-water flow seems to be between about 10,000 and 18,000 cfs, although some of the rapids get more difficult as the flows drop below 10,000.

The white water below Kerr Dam and Buffalo Bridge consists of four major rapids with some minor white water between. The first rapid, known as The Ledge, comes about a mile downstream from the put-in, where the river takes a big bend. Here a horizontal band of rock crosses the river, creating a small drop with some holes and waves. While The Ledge washes out at flows much over 15,000 cfs, it can be very

Negotiating a rocky white-water stretch of the Middle Fork of the Flathead River. Hank Fischer photo.

Bouncing down the Buffalo Rapids on the Flathead River. Glacier Raft Co. photo.

difficult when the river is low—some think even tougher than Buffalo itself.

Next, about a half mile downstream, comes Pinball, an area where large rocks in the river create a hazard. At very low flows, it's a rock-dodging course, and you may find yourself careening from one rock to another. At more normal flows, the rocks disappear and some big waves develop, as well as at least one tricky hole. This one can wash out at high flows.

Then another quarter mile downstream comes Eagle Wave Rapid, the longest continuous white water of the run, and perhaps the most interesting. At low flows, it's a rather technical rapid with lots of rocks showing and some fast channels. At higher flows, a long set of standing waves develops that makes for good fun.

The final piece of white water is Buffalo Rapids itself, generally recognized as the most difficult. It's a long S-turn, with the water first sweeping left and then right. There are at least two major obstacles—a diagonal wave and a big rock at a narrow point—that should be scouted if it's your first trip through. It's not hard to recognize Buffalo, as the river narrows markedly and the cliffs get higher. There's an easy eddy to hit on the left side of the river immediately above the rapid, and there's a good path up to the cliffs for an excellent view of the river. Buffalo Rapids is really ideal at about 15,000 cfs; at this flow, look out for a big wave in the bottom part of the run. Many rafters make the big climb up this wall of water, stall out in the vertical position, and flip over. The obvious line through Buffalo runs down the left channel, and almost everyone runs it that way; it's much more hazardous on the right. After Buffalo there are a couple miles of flat water before hitting the takeout at Buffalo Bridge.

While the Buffalo Rapids aren't particularly difficult—strong intermediates will do fine—they can be hazardous because of the high water volume and strong currents. The rapids are mostly Class II and Class III, with Buffalo itself a very strong Class III at certain flows.

It is possible to get information on water levels by calling the Montana Power Office at Kerr Dam (833-4450); try first thing in the morning as people are in and out at other times. Be forewarned, however, that MPC only provides *current* flows, and generally cannot provide a forecast; actual levels can vary significantly between morning and evening.

Floater use of the Buffalo Rapids has increased markedly over the past decade. According to recreation officials with the Confederated Salish and Kootenai Tribes, peak days may see as many as 200 people on the river. For those interested in commercial trips, the Glacier Raft Company generally runs two trips per day on this section; call 883-5838 in Polson.

Gallatin River

The upper 40 miles of the West Gallatin River contain some of Montana's very finest white water with an abundance of technical rapids, tight turns, big rocks, and large waves. While much of Montana's white water consists of single rapids separated by long stretches of flat water, the Gallatin distinguishes itself with its quantity of white water as well as its quality; on some stretches there is near-continuous action. Almost all of Gallatin's white water is easily accessible, as the river not only flows primarily through public land but is also generally close to Highway 191. Even though the Gallatin is a relatively small river, it can maintain good boating well into the summer.

The white-water action on the Gallatin starts right where the river leaves Yellowstone National Park; be aware that boating is not permitted inside the park boundary. This upper section, from the park boundary to Big Sky, where the West Fork flows in, can be handled by intermediate rafters and strong intermediate canoeists during high water; it's typically broad and shallow with some tight turns. It's rated as a Class II run, but watch out for the big waves. A standard run on this upper section is from the Forest Service's Red Cliff access six miles downstream to Big Sky. The river is rarely run above Red Cliff. Typically this upper section of river is only floatable until about mid-July. Watch out for downed trees.

As the West Gallatin churns downstream, it becomes increasingly more difficult. The next section, from Big Sky to Greek Creek, is about nine miles long and features several tight turns and challenging rapids as the river quickly picks up volume. There's a particularly challenging spot near where Portal Creek spills in. While intermediate rafters can generally handle this section, canoeists should be very strong intermediates. It's mostly Class II water with some Class III.

The next section of the Gallatin, between Greek Creek and the Squaw Creek Bridge, is where the really heavy-duty Gallatin white water lies. Not long after Greek Creek, as the canyon grows narrower, the river changes once again, with more tight turns, more rocks in the river, more continuous white water, and fewer eddies where it's easy to pull out and bail or take a break.

Between Greek Creek and the Cascade Creek Bridge (also known as the 35-mile-per-hour bridge) lie several tricky rapids, including a local favorite known as Screaming Left Turn and a tricky keeper called Hilarity Hole. While the rapids can be intense—this section rates a solid Class III—the most difficult white water comes between Cascade Creek and the Squaw Creek Bridge. This final two miles is for experts only during high water, so don't miss the takeout at Cascade Creek (on the left side of the river, opposite the highway) if you don't have those skills.

Below the Cascade Creek Bridge the white water is nearly continuous, with big rocks and big water as the river is narrowly constricted. This section contains the Gallatin's most famous white water—House Rock Rapid—and immediately after the rock comes a boulder field and a run known as the Mad Mile. Again, this section is for properly equipped experts, running in groups. Super-expert canoeists have run this section in recent years, but it requires a great deal of flotation and really exceptional skills. This

House Rock Rapids on the West Gallatin. U.S. Forest Service photo.

section contains many Class III rapids and a few Class IV runs.

There's one more good stretch of white water after Squaw Creek that runs for about eight miles to the highway bridge at the mouth of Gallatin Canyon. This section has some very good Class III water and is quite popular. Watch out for a weir a couple of miles below Squaw Creek; at higher flows it's possible to run over it, but beware of a big standing wave at the bottom.

While the Gallatin was chiefly the domain of kayakers for many years, recently rafters and canoeists have taken to the river in greater numbers. Farther down the canyon where the river is narrower, floating can be possible well into the summer, and dodging rocks presents an entirely new set of challenges. For information on water levels, call the Yellowstone Raft Company (995-4613) at Big Sky or the Northern Lights Trading Company (586-2338) in Bozeman; the Yellowstone Raft Company does daily trips on the river and always has up-to-date river information.

Madison River

The white-water action on the Madison River lies in Bear Trap Canyon, on a 10-mile long section of river that runs through the Bear Trap Canyon Wilderness, a 6,000-acre area managed by the Bureau of Land Management. The 1,500-foot-high cliffs that border the river serve as the backdrop for one of Montana's most scenic white-water trips.

The canyon starts at the outlet to Ennis Lake and continues until Highway 84 meets the river. The dirt road and put-in point at the head of Bear Trap Canyon are both on Montana Power Company land, but Montana Power has been very cooperative with access. This narrow dirt road can be rather hazardous, so drive slowly; there's

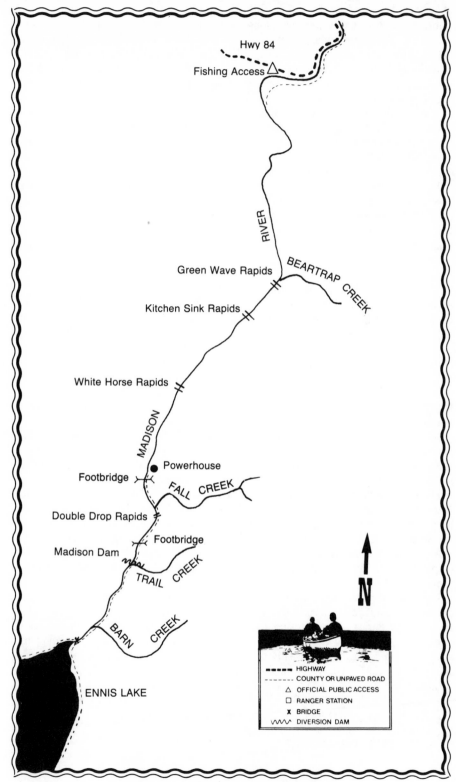

Bear Trap Canyon

a designated parking area to relieve congestion. The standard takeout point at the bottom of the canyon lies immediately off Highway 84 where Warm Springs Creek meets the Madison. This site is privately owned, so be sure not to litter or make a mess.

While water flows on the Madison are regulated by both the Madison Dam and the Hebgen Dam, neither are storage reservoirs. So when there's a high influx of water, it gets passed through. Flows vary from 900 to 10,000 cubic feet per second based on the season. Optimal flow for floating activities is about 1,500 to 2,200 cfs. The Bureau of Land Management pulls its river ranger off the river when flows get over 2,500 cfs. The river gets exceedingly dangerous when flows hit the 4,000 to 5,000 cfs level. About 200 yards upstream from the powerhouse is a river flow sign, updated daily, which indicates current water levels in the canyon.

The Bear Trap is characterized by several intense rapids with considerable stretches of easy water between. There are four primary rapids, and all have unmarked portage routes for those not along for the thrills. The first white water is Double Drop Rapids, which you'll miss if you put in too close to the powerhouse. The next major white water, White Horse Rapids, comes about two miles below the powerhouse. It's a long set of big waves.

After White Horse comes the most difficult and dangerous rapids in the Bear Trap, the Kitchen Sink. It has large waves, some big drops, lots of rocks, and two turns. A wave that lurches back over a large rock at the bottom of the run—which some people think looks like a drain at the bottom of a sink—gives this rapid its name. According to BLM, at least eight people have lost their lives in the Kitchen Sink rapids over the past 20 years. At peak flows, it clearly presents a life-threatening situation. The danger of this rapid is accentuated by its remoteness; it's just about in the middle of the canyon.

The last major white water is known either as Green Wave Rapids or The Dumplings, and it's a series of huge rocks in the river which some creative mind decided looks like chicken dumplings floating in a bowl of broth. These rapids lie about three miles before the takeout point.

As on most large rivers, quality equipment is critical. Equally important are experience and judgment. Only strong intermediates should normally try the Bear Trap, and experts should try only experts when the water is up. While most of the water is Class II or III, the Kitchen Sink is a Class IV rapid at lower flows, and at higher levels is a Class V. It's a very tricky, very dangerous piece of white water that people without the proper skill level simply shouldn't attempt. There's been a historical problem with beginners in small paddle boats wearing horse-collar life jackets taking on the Bear Trap. Carefully evaluate your ability and equipment before making this run. Several outfitters run trips in the Bear Trap if you want to check it out with experienced people first. The most experienced are the people at the Yellowstone Raft Company; call 995-4613 in Big Sky.

The Bear Trap has a few hazards other than tough white water. Rattlesnakes inhabit the canyon, and if you believe all the stories, they're commoner than earthworms. Ticks are numerous during spring and summer months, so check your hair and clothes. Poison oak is also found in the canyon; it's characterized by shiny green leaves in groups of three. Still want to go? Occasionally grizzly bears use the canyon during the summer, as do black bears. Give them some distance and keep your food well secured.

Boaters will be pleased to know the Bureau of Land Management has published an excellent floater's guide to Bear Trap Canyon. It not only provides good information, but has an excellent topographic map with photographs of the approaches to the four major rapids. It's available free of charge by writing to the Bureau of Land Management, Box 3388, Butte, MT 59702.

For information on water conditions, call the Yellowstone Raft Company in Big Sky or the Bureau of Land Management in Butte (494-5059).

Middle Fork of the Flathead

The Middle Fork of the Flathead is one of Montana's most wild and remote whitewater rivers. While the wilderness section or the Middle Fork is renowned for its difficult rapids, the more accessible portion of the river immediately adjacent to Glacier National Park also has outstanding white water.

As might be expected, access to the wilderness portion of the Middle Fork is quite difficult. The options are either to pack in with horses or fly in to the airstrip at Schafer Meadows; most people do the latter. Flying in provides an interesting perspective on the river. It appears as a tiny thread of water that is liberally sprinkled with large boulders and occasional logjams. Trees in the river are particularly hazardous in the upper sections of the river, so watch out.

While the logjams and rapids are obstacles everyone usually anticipates, the single biggest problem that many people overlook is the lethal combination of cold weather and cold water temperatures. It's not unusual to have a cold rain falling during early-season Middle Fork trips, and if you don't have a wetsuit or good rain gear, hypothermia becomes a real possibility. Hypothermia can then lead to serious errors in judgment, like not wanting to stop and scout difficult rapids. Be prepared for cold temperatures and adverse weather.

Flows on the Middle Fork are highly variable. While the average low flows are around 1,000 cubic feet of water per second (measured at West Glacier), peak flows can be more than 10 times that amount. When the river is really high, even the professional outfitters don't go.

Major rapids on the Middle Fork begin only a couple of miles below Schafer Meadows, with a group known as the Three Forks series; they're rated by the Forest

White water on the Middle Fork of the Flathead. Carol Fischer photo.

Middle Fork of the Flathead River near Spruce Park. Carol Fischer photo.

Service at high flows at Class IV; at normal flow they're a Class III.

These three rapids are all within about a one-mile stretch upstream from Morrison Creek. There are a couple more rapids, easily seen and scouted in advance, before hitting the toughest rapids on the Middle Fork, the Spruce Park series, which start just downstream from the Spruce Park guard station. The rapids have some huge waves, big rocks, and turbulence capable of flipping a raft. They're rated by the Forest Service as Class V at peak flows, but under more normal conditions they are a solid Class IV. You'll want to check these out carefully before going through, but be advised that the terrain and continuous white water makes scouting rather difficult in some places.

There aren't any more difficult rapids until the Middle Fork meets Highway 2 near Bear Creek. Just downstream from Bear Creek, near the goat lick adjacent to the Isaac Walton Lodge lie a couple more rapids, though they aren't nearly as tough as the Spruce Park rapids; they're rated as Class III.

While there's occasional white water between the Essex Bridge and Nyack, it's mostly Class II. Do watch for a drop called Brown's Hole, about a mile below Paola Creek; it can be difficult at high water. Intermediate canoeists can handle this section, except at high flows. It's a strikingly beautiful section of river.

The next white water comes between Nyack and West Glacier in the John Stevens Canyon. Here the river is restricted to a narrow thread as it drops rapidly over rock ledges. It drops about 35 feet per mile as it dashes through the canyon. The run lasts for about five miles and has fairly continuous white water through the middle of the canyon.

For those who like to know the names of the rapids, here's the rundown for the John Stevens Canyon: The first two, Tunnel and Bonecrusher, are pretty mild; they get you ready for the toughest rapid, known as Jaws. Next comes Waterfall, then Narrows, then C.B.T., and then shortly before West Glacier, Pumphouse. Most of the rapids are Class II or III, but the Forest Service rates Jaws as Class IV at peak flows.

Good intermediate rafters can handle the Middle Fork downstream from Bear Creek. Because of its isolation in the upper section, it's recommended for experts only. Check with the Flathead National Forest office in Hungry Horse (387-5243) for up-to-date water conditions and information on hazards.

Stillwater River

With nearly 40 miles of high-quality white water, the Stillwater contains as many rapids as any river in Montana. Although the stream is relatively small, it offers some extremely difficult water, particularly in the upper reaches.

White-water action can start at the end of the road near the Woodbine campground, where the water is extremely formidable. This is the site of the Woodbine Rapids, which run for about a mile and contain some very difficult Class IV water as well as one Class V drop; in high water, it's deemed unrunnable. There's nearly continuous white water for the next mile and a half before hitting Chrome Mine Rapids, opposite from the old mine. This difficult spot lasts about 300 yards and is a bona fide Class V rapid; only a small number of people have run this spot. Like Woodbine, this rapid is unrunnable at peak flows; it starts out with an eight-foot waterfall and stays tough with many rocks and a dashing flow. An upset in this rapid spells extreme punishment if not death. This entire three-mile section is only for the best of the experts; it may well be the toughest three miles of white water in Montana.

After the Chrome Mine Rapids, the river calms down for the next nine miles before it reaches the access point at Moraine; this is almost all Class I and II water. The eight-mile stretch of river between Moraine and Cliffswallow access points is one of the most popular, as it contains an abundance of white water, mostly Class III but some Class IV. The section is characterized by sharp turns and several abrupt drops. The biggest rapids are named after nearby access points: first comes the Moraine Rapids, then the Castle Rock Rapids, and finally the Roscoe Rapids about two miles upstream from Cliffswallow. You'll want to stop and scout all of these spots. This section of river is suited for advanced intermediates and experts.

Boaters should be aware of several low bridges that span the river in the section between Moraine and Cliffswallow. At high flows, these bridges can be too low for rafts to pass under; kayakers sometimes roll to get under if they don't want to carry around. Be sure to watch ahead. Boaters on all sections should be aware of logs and other debris that tend to build up around bridge pilings during high water. Such debris may block passage for much of the river.

After the Cliffswallow access the serious rapids subside, and good intermediate canoeists can try their skills. It's about an eight-mile run to Absarokee, with mostly strong Class II water.

It's the same story from Absarokee down to the Whitebird access: some good white water, but nothing outrageous, most just solid Class II water. The final standard run is the four-mile trip between Whitebird and the Fireman's Point access site. Again, it's primarily Class II water, but look out for a decent drop with a big wave about half a mile downstream from Whitebird; at high flows it can be very hazardous for canoeists. All of the river between the Cliffswallow access and Fireman's Point is good intermediate canoeing water except at peak flows.

In an average year, the upper Stillwater—above Absarokee—usually gets too low by mid-July. The lower river usually holds up throughout the summer.

While the Stillwater has typically been used primarily by kayakers, more rafters and canoeists have been using the river in recent years. The upper Stillwater has some very challenging rafting water that's similar to the West Gallatin; while it might not be quite as difficult, it's perhaps slightly more continuous. It's only a matter of time before people from Billings discover the outstanding water. Once again, however, rafters should be very wary of the low bridges between Moraine and Cliffswallow access points; at peak flows, they're a real hazard.

For those interested in trying some boating on the Stillwater, a group from Billings known as the Beartooth Paddler's Society extends an open invitation for people to show up at the Moraine or Cliffswallow access points on nearly any Saturday or Sunday during the peak floating season (usually about mid-May to mid-July). It's a good opportunity to go down the river with experienced people. It's tough for inexperienced people to get started on the Stillwater, as there aren't any professional outfitters who do the white water commercially.

Yellowstone River

While the Yellowstone is better known for its fishing and wildlife, both Yankee Jim Canyon and a stretch of river below Gardiner offer good white-water excitement. A relatively short run lasting only about four miles, Yankee Jim Canyon starts about 13 miles downstream from Gardiner; access is easy, as the river never gets too far from the highway. At normal summer flows it's not a particularly difficult run, although at high water it gets extremely challenging because of the tremendous water volume and the narrow constriction of the canyon.

Proximity to the highway and several pieces of Gallatin National Forest land near the river make access fairly easy. The first standard access point is an undeveloped put-in right at the town of Gardiner. There's some excellent white water between Gardiner and Corwin Springs that has become increasingly popular in recent years. While not overwhelmingly difficult—it's all solid Class II water except at peak flows when some Class III water develops—this section of river has a steep gradient, contains many rocks and has quite a few sharp turns. There are more rapids here than in Yankee Jim, and it's a favored spot for kayakers as well as intermediate canoeists.

The best of the white water between Gardiner and Corwin Springs can be found in the first three or four miles; there's a Forest Service access site about three miles north of Gardiner just past the airstrip that's often used as a take-out.

Many Yellowstone white-water trips start near Corwin Springs, where there are two public access points. For the first four or five miles, however, it's mostly flat water, although the scenery is outstanding as the river winds through the mountains. For those interested only in white water, a Forest Service access point called the Joe Brown Trail lies just upstream from the start of Yankee Jim Canyon. It's the last access before the white water starts, with the standard takeout point about four miles downstream at the Tom Miner Bridge. Although most people don't realize it, the takeout at Tom Miner Bridge is privately owned, so be considerate. There is a publicly owned access only a quarter-mile below Tom Miner Bridge at Carbella.

Yankee Jim Canyon is not particularly difficult in late July and August when the water is low; intermediates can handle it then with little trouble. But those who do the river at low flows will find it markedly different than at peak flows, when the rapids are much larger and more difficult. At this time, at least two of the rapids can become Class IV. However, at more normal flows none of the rapids in Yankee Jim rate higher than Class III, and they may be only Class II at low flows. While there have been drownings in Yankee Jim during the past decade, they've been the result of inexperience and no life jackets—a fatal combination. Those interested in up-to-date water conditions can call the Crazy Mountain Company in Emigrant (333-4779) or the Yellowstone Raft Company in Gardiner (848-7777), two local outfitting companies that work the river regularly.

Yankee Jim Canyon consists of three major rapids. The first is known either as Yankee

Jim's Revenge or Boateater Rapid, and according to outfitters who frequent the river, it flips more boats than any other rapid.

When the water is high, the Revenge consists of a long tongue of water that leads directly into a huge standing wave. If boaters aren't set up right for the wave, it's swimtime. This rapid has a reputation for taking the unwary by surprise.

The second major rapid is the easily identified Big Rock Rapid. As one might guess, it consists of a huge rock in the middle of the river. While not technically difficult, in high water a dangerous hole forms behind the rock, and in very high water, when the river goes over the rock, a large standing wave develops. Under more normal conditions, it's a straight shot past the rock.

The final major white water in the canyon is known as the Boxcar Rapids. At high water, it's generally considered the toughest, and some outfitters believe it's unrunnable at extremely high flows. The river constricts very narrowly at this point, and huge standing waves develop; the higher the water, the higher the waves.

The lesson of Yankee Jim is not much different than most Montana white water: be aware that conditions change dramatically with spring runoff. For instance, while in August the river may move at a pleasant three miles per hour and hit temperatures of 60 degrees or more, in June the river may be roaring at seven miles per hour with a temperature in the upper 30s. Keep in mind that it's hard to define an "average" year; runoff may extend late into July.

Who will speak for the rivers?

"The rivers are our brothers. They quench our thirst. They carry our canoes and feed our children... and you must henceforth give the rivers the kindness you would give any brother." —Chief Seattle of the Duwamish Indians

Montana is blessed to have so many free-flowing and undisturbed rivers. The Treasure State's growth has lagged behind the rest of the country, and the forces that have killed many of America's spectacular waterways have been slow to reach Montana. Now, however, the threats to Montana's rivers are building; energy development, dams, streamside subdivision, water depletion, and pollution hang like dark clouds over these sparkling streams.

Human overuse is one of the few problems which most Montana streams do not face today. The question, then, is: why write a floater's guide? If floating in Montana becomes more popular, managing agencies may be forced to limit the number of floaters and impose certain restrictions. This has already happened in other Western states, including Idaho, Utah, and Oregon.

The answer is simple. Limiting the number of boats going down a river is easy compared to preventing impoundment, channelization, depletion, or pollution of wild waterways. It takes overwhelming public pressure to deny such tragedies. Rivers have no voice of their own, so concerned citizens must speak for them. Time and again, the people who use the rivers—and thus know their value—arise as their defenders.

There are several important aspects of river protection. First of all, it's essential to ensure that an adequate amount of water remains instream, not only for floating, but to protect fish and wildlife and maintain water quality. Several of Montana's most outstanding rivers—including the Big Hole, Jefferson, Bitterroot, Sun, and Beaverhead—suffer from serious dewatering.

State law does permit state agencies to file for instream flows to protect fish and wildlife, recreation, and water quality. The Montana Board of Natural Resources decides if the amount of water requested for instream uses is necessary to protect the resource. Only the Yellowstone River and its tributaries have gone through this extensive water allocation process. Who gets the water in many of Montana's rivers will be decided in the near future. When this process begins, citizens must become involved so that industrial and agricultural interests don't predominate. Watch for notices of public hearings.

In addition to maintaining adequate instream flows, the shorelines and the river itself need protection from inappropriate development. Besides becoming eyesores for floaters, streamside subdivisions provide the impetus for riprapping, channelization, and levees. These problems can be attacked on a local level by regulating building activities in the floodplain. Contact your county commissioners.

Another method, which has been used successfully on the Blackfoot River, is

128

Libby Dam. Lance Schelvan photo.

Stream channelization ruins fish habitat, water quality, and floating.
Department of Fish, Wildlife and Parks photo.

Car body rip-rap along the Bitterroot. Hank Fischer photo.

cooperative management. Landowners, concerned citizens, and appropriate state agencies get together and work out agreements whereby the river corridor is preserved and opened to carefully managed recreation. In areas where local landowners are strongly concerned about protecting natural values, this system has real potential.

Montana has no state wild and scenic rivers program. While there are laws which afford the streambed itself modest protection, the state has no means of protecting segments of rivers that have outstanding natural values.

This is where the National Wild and Scenic Rivers System fits in. Montana currently has four federally designated "wild and scenic" rivers: the three forks of the Flathead and a 149-mile section of the Missouri River. While many Montana rivers have been proposed for designation by citizens (the Madison and Yellowstone rivers were even temporarily part of a congressional study bill in 1978), this concept has met staunch resistance from Montana landowners who worry that such designations may unduly impact both private and public lands. Those concerned about Montana's rivers—both those who live in-state and out—should let their congressmen know these rivers are a *national* resource that merit federal protection.

Those concerned about the future of Montana's rivers should help support the efforts of citizens' organizations working to protect them. Although Montana has no single organization that deals exclusively with rivers, the Montana Environmental Information Center, the Montana Wilderness Association, and the Montana Wildlife Federation are three statewide groups that deal with river issues. National organizations such as Trout Unlimited, Defenders of Wildlife, Sierra Club, National Audubon Society, American Rivers Conservation Council, American League of Anglers, and the National Wildlife Federation have also been involved and deserve support.

Most often, however, the work is handled by local citizens, who seem to pop up like mushrooms when they learn their river is threatened. These organizations always need help, both physical and financial. Lend a hand so that future generations have the same opportunities to enjoy clean and free rivers that you've had.

Appendix I: Conservation organizations

Montana Environmental
Information Center
  Box 1184
  Helena MT 59624

Montana Wilderness Association
  Box 635
  Helena, MT 59624

Montana Wildlife Federation
  Box 3526
  Bozeman, MT 59715

Trout Unlimited
  501 Church St., NE
  Vienna, VA 22180

Defenders of Wildlife
  1244 Nineteenth St., NW
  Washington, DC 20036

Sierra Club
  730 Polk St.
  San Francisco, CA 94109

National Audubon Society
  950 Third Avenue
  New York, NY 10022

American Rivers Conservation Council
  322 4th St., NE
  Washington, DC 20002

National Wildlife Federation
  1412 16th St., NW
  Washington, DC 20036

American League of Anglers
  810 Eighteenth St., NW
  Washington, DC 20036

American Wilderness Alliance
  7600 E. Arapahoe Rd.
  Suite 114
  Englewood, CO 80112

The Wilderness Society
  1400 I St., NW, 10th Floor
  Washington, DC 20005

Appendix II: Stream access

This appendix summarizes how Montana's new stream-access law, passed in 1985, affects the recreational use of the state's streams and rivers.

Water classification

Please read carefully the following definitions as they are important in determining the recreational uses that require permission.

Class I waters are defined as those which are capable of recreational use and have been declared navigable or which are capable of specific kinds of commercial activity, including commercial outfitting with multiperson watercraft. The Montana Department of Fish, Wildlife and Parks has developed a preliminary list of rivers that meet at least one of the criteria listed in the law for Class I rivers. This preliminary list includes the mainstems of the following waters, as described:

Kootenai River Drainage: Kootenai River—from Libby Dam to the Idaho border; Lake Creek—from the Chase cut-off road to its confluence with the Kootenai River; Yaak River—from Yaak Falls to its confluence with the Kootenai River.

Flathead River Drainage: South Fork of the Flathead—from Youngs Creek to Hungry Horse Reservoir; Middle Fork of the Flathead—from Schaffer Creek to its confluence with the mainstem of the Flathead River; North Fork of the Flathead—from the Canadian border to its confluence with the mainstem of the Flathead River; Flathead River (mainstem)—to its confluence with the Clark Fork River.

Clark Fork of the Columbia River Drainage: Clark Fork River—from Warm Spring Creek to the Idaho border; North Fork of the Blackfoot—from Highway 200 east of Ovando to its confluence with the mainstem of the Blackfoot River; Blackfoot River—from the Cedar Meadow Fishing Access Site west of Helmville to its confluence with the Clark Fork; Bitterroot River—from the confluence of the East and West forks to its confluence with the Clark Fork; Rock Creek—from the confluence of the West Fork to its confluence with the Clark Fork.

Missouri River Drainage: Missouri River—from Three Forks to the North Dakota border; Beaverhead River—from Clark Canyon Dam to its confluence with the Jefferson; Big Hole River—from Fishtrap Fishing Access Site downstream from Wisdom to its confluence with the Jefferson; Gallatin River—from Taylors Fork to its confluence with the Missouri; Jefferson River—to its confluence with the Missouri; Madison River—from Quake Lake to its confluence with the Missouri; Dearborn

River—from the Highway 434 bridge to its confluence with the Missouri; Sun River—from Gibson Dam to its confluence with the Missouri; Smith River—from Camp Baker Fishing Access Site near Fort Logan to its confluence with the Missouri; Marias River—from Tiber Dam to its confluence with the Missouri; Judith River—from the confluence of Big Spring Creek to its confluence with the Missouri.

Yellowstone River Drainage: Yellowstone River—from Yellowstone National Park to the North Dakota border; Bighorn River—from Yellowtail Dam to its confluence with the Yellowstone; Tongue River—from Tongue River Dam to its confluence with the Yellowstone.

Keep in mind that this list is preliminary and that other waters may be added to it in the future as other criteria listed in the law for determining Class I waters are addressed. Also, keep in mind that there may be times during a year when the flow and physical condition of these waters may not permit their use for certain kinds of recreation.

Class II waters are all rivers and streams capable of recreational use that are not Class I waters.

What types of activities require landowner permission?

On *both* Class I and Class II waters, landowner permission is required for the following recreational uses, even if these activities take place between the high-water marks:

• Operating all-terrain vehicles or other motorized vehicles not intended for use on the water;

• Making recreational use of stock ponds or private impoundments fed by intermittent streams. Although this restriction deals specifically with only those stock ponds or impoundments fed by intermittent streams, it's recommended, as a matter of courtesy, that recreationists obtain permission from landowners before using any private ponds;

• Making recreational use of water diverted away from a stream, such as an irrigation canal or drainage ditch.

• Big game hunting (the Fish and Game Commission may specifically authorize hunting only by shotgun or longbow and arrow between the ordinary high-water marks without landowner permission);

• Overnight camping within sight of, or within 500 yards of an occupied dwelling (whichever is less). Even if permission is obtained, recreationists must stay within the ordinary high-water marks unless arrangements have been made with the landowner;

• The placement or creation of any permanent duck blind, boat moorage, or any seasonal or other objects within sight of, or within 500 yards of, an occupied dwelling (whichever is less);

• Using a streambed as a right-of-way for any purpose when no water is flowing.

In addition, on *all* Class II waters, the following activities require landowner permission:

• Big game hunting;

• Overnight camping;

• The placement or creation of any seasonal objects such as a duck blind;

• Any other pleasure activities *not primarily water related.*

These restrictions apply on streams flowing through privately owned land. Of course, if the landowner grants permission for any of the activities mentioned, they would be permitted. Recreation on public lands may take place in accordance with the regulations of the agencies managing these lands.

Portage

The new law states that recreationists using a stream may go above the ordinary high-water mark to portage around barriers, but must do so in the least intrusive manner possible, avoiding damage to the landowner's property and violation of his rights. *Barrier* is defined as an artificial obstruction in or over the water which totally or effectively obstructs the recreational use of the surface water. *The new law does not address portage around natural barriers, and does not make such a portage either legal or illegal.*

If a landowner puts a fence or other structure across a stream, such as a float-over cable or a float-through gate, and it does not interfere with the recreational use of the water, the public does not have the right to go above the ordinary high-water mark to portage. In all cases, recreationists are encouraged to keep portages to a minimum, and they should realize that landowners may place fences and other barriers across streams for purposes of land or water management or to establish land ownership, if otherwise allowed by law.

Portage routes

The law sets out a process by which either a landowner or a member of the public may, if necessary, request that a portage route over or around a barrier be established. The Department of Fish, Wildlife and Parks encourages, however, that portage problems be solved through other means if at all possible. If establishing a portage route is deemed the only workable solution, the request would have to be submitted to the board of supervisors of the local conservation or grazing district, or to the board of county commissioners. For assistance in determining where to file a request, or for other information regarding portage-route establishment, maintenance and signing, contact the Montana Department of Fish, Wildlife and Parks' Portage Coordinator at (406) 444-5667.

Liability

The Legislature has limited the situations in which a landowner may be liable for injuries to people using a stream flowing through his property. This limitation on liability applies not only to the landowner, but also to his agent or tenant and to supervisors who participate in a decision regarding a portage route. The new law states that landowners and others covered by the restriction on liability are liable only for acts or omissions that constitute "willful or wanton misconduct."

Prescriptive easements and land title

The Legislature stated that a prescriptive easement cannot be acquired through recreational use of rivers and streams, the beds and banks, portage routes or property crossed to reach streams. It also said that the new law does not affect title to surface waters, including the beds and banks of any rivers or streams, or portage routes used by the public.

Appendix III: Finding maps

There are four basic sources for floaters who want detailed maps of rivers and the surrounding lands: the Bureau of Land Management (BLM), the Forest Service (FS), the Montana Department of Fish, Wildlife and Parks (DFW&P), and the U.S. Geological Survey (USGS). While USGS provides the most detailed maps, the most useful maps other than regular floater's maps are the standard BLM and FS maps. These maps have an advantage over USGS maps because of their smaller scale and the fact that they show land ownership patterns, roads, trails, and access points.

The BLM's relatively new map series, "Public Lands in Montana," may well be the best maps. These 42 maps cover almost all of Montana, with a few exceptions. These maps are especially useful because they block up to one another. They currently cost $1 each and are available at all BLM offices or by writing to the BLM State Office, Box 30157, Billings, MT 59107. The scale is one-half inch per mile and the maps show roads, trails, streams, lakes, and recreation sites.

The BLM has another map series that's helpful for several rivers not covered by FS maps or the standard BLM maps. It's known as the 1:100,000 series, and the maps are available for $3.25 each by writing to the BLM State Office in Billings; they are sometimes available at local BLM offices as well. Be advised that these maps are not nearly as detailed as the "Public Lands in Montana" series; many of the secondary roads and access points aren't shown. Of maps listed under each river, they're generally the least desirable.

The BLM plans to phase out its outstanding "Public Lands in Montana" series starting in 1986, although it will take 10 years or more to completely changeover. The plan is to start a new map series, similar to the 1:100,000 series, but with more detail concerning secondary roads and recreation sites. The first maps of this new series, scheduled for production in 1986, will replace the Breaks (#16) and U.L. Bend (#17) maps of the "Public Lands in Montana" series. Slated for production in 1987 will be Pryor (#36) and Haxby (#18). The "Public Lands in Montana" series will continue to be printed and used until new maps are developed to replace them.

The Forest Service has now completed its Forest Visitors Series maps. Each map covers one national forest or a part of a national forest (some large forests have more than one map); they have essentially the same features as the BLM maps. These maps cost $1 apiece and are available at most Forest Service offices or by writing to the U.S. Forest Service, Box 7669, Missoula, MT 59807. Make your check for the amount of purchase only; it's not necessary to include postage. The Forest Service also has maps available of existing wilderness areas for $1 as well. The Forest Service maps are also on a scale of one-half inch per mile. The annoying thing about the FS maps is that they only show the portions of the rivers on the forest, and the forests often don't block up to one another, leaving large blank spaces with no Forest Service map coverage.

Some agencies, such as the Montana Department of Fish, Wildlife, and Parks, are beginning to prepare maps especially for river recreationists. These maps—such as ones for the Blackfoot, the Smith, and the Yellowstone—are generally exceptionally helpful and of very high quality. In addition, the DFW&P publishes a "Montana Recreation Guide," a map of Montana that shows all state fishing access sites (usually good launch sites), recreation areas, and state parks. Pick one up at any regional office or by writing to Montana Department of Fish, Wildlife and Parks, 1420 East Sixth, Helena, MT 59601. The guide is free.

For those who want more detail than the FS or BLM maps provide, or for those sections of rivers that just can't be found elsewhere, USGS topographic maps are the best bet. An index for these maps is printed on both BLM and FS maps. You can send your request and $2.50 for each map to U.S. Geological Survey, Box 25286, Denver, CO 80225. The scale of these maps is 2.64 inches per mile, so they can be a bit bulky if you're planning a long trip—it may take four or five maps to cover a 30-mile section of river. Be prepared to cut and paste. Such maps are usually available locally from drafting or blueprint offices or sporting goods stores.

Here's a river-by-river listing of the maps I've found useful when floating Montana rivers:

Beaverhead River. BLM Dillon (#32) map covers the entire river; Beaverhead National Forest Map (known as the Interagency Travel Plan and Visitors Map, Southwestern Montana) covers entire river.

Blackfoot River. Montana DFW&P has excellent Blackfoot River guide available for free by writing to DFW&P at 3201 Spurgin Road, Missoula, MT 59801. Lolo National Forest maps show entire river; BLM Granite (#21) map shows part of lower river; BLM Avon (#22) map shows part of upper river; FS Flathead National Forest map (south half) and Lewis and Clark National Forest map (Rocky Mountain Division) and Helena National Forest map show the upper Blackfoot, above Clearwater Junction.

Big Hole River. BLM Dillon (#32) and Big Hole (#31) maps cover entire river; Beaverhead National Forest map covers entire river; FS Deer Lodge National Forest map covers from a few miles above Wise River to Glen.

Bighorn River. Good maps are hard to find for the Bighorn. Best bet is the BLM 1:100,000 series (#80 and #81), which covers all except for the last 10 miles of the river. BLM Public Lands in Montana Sumatra map (#27) covers the last 10 miles.

Bitterroot River. FS Bitterroot National Forest map shows entire river; BLM 1:100,000 series (#'s 13, 14, and 15) show entire river.

Clark Fork River. BLM Granite (#21) and Avon (#22) maps cover the river above Missoula; FS Deer Lodge National Forest covers upper Clark Fork above Rock Creek; FS Lolo National Forest maps cover entire river below Rock Creek. BLM 1:100,000 series (#7 and #12) cover lower river.

Dearborn River. Good maps hard to find. BLM 1:100,000 series (#30 and #40) covers entire river. FS Lewis and Clark National Forest map (Rocky Mountain Division) shows the upper Dearborn to just below the Highway 200 bridge.

Flathead River (main branch). Flathead National Forest maps (both north half and south half) show river to just below Buffalo Bridge; BLM 1:100,000 series (maps #11 and #12) shows entire river below Flathead Lake; fair lower Flathead map available from the Wilderness Institute, University of Montana, Missoula, MT 59812.

Middle Fork of the Flathead. The Flathead National Forest and Glacier National Park have jointly produced a special waterproof floater's map entitled "Three Forks of the Flathead River." It provides a great deal of information as well as locations of rapids, access points, etc. The map is available at a cost of $2 from the Flathead National Forest, Box 147, Kalispell, MT 59901. Flathead National Forest map (south half) shows entire river; Flathead National Forest map (north half) shows river to just below Spruce Park. USGS map of Glacier Park shows river below Bear Creek.

North Fork of the Flathead. See information under Middle Fork of Flathead concerning special floater's map. Forest Service Flathead National Forest map (north half) shows entire river; USGS Glacier National Park map shows entire river.

South Fork of the Flathead. See information under Middle Fork of Flathead concerning special floater's map. Forest Service Flathead National Forest map (south half) shows river below Salmon Forks; Forest Service Bob Marshall Wilderness map shows the river above Spotted Bear.

Gallatin River. BLM Madison (#33) map covers entire river; FS Gallatin National Forest map covers West Fork of Madison to Shedds Bridge.

Jefferson River. BLM Dillon (#32) and Madison (#33) maps cover entire river; FS Beaverhead National Forest map covers river upstream from Cardwell; FS Deer Lodge National Forest map covers river downstream to just past Lewis and Clark Caverns.

Kootenai River. FS Kootenai National Forest map covers entire river. BLM 1:100,000 series (maps #4 and #5) cover entire river.

Madison River. BLM Madison (#33) map covers the river from the West Madison recreation area downstream; FS Gallatin National Forest map covers the river from Yellowstone Park to Greycliffs. BLM has special Bear Trap Canyon Floater's Guide: USGS map with rapids marked and river information. Available for free by writing to the Bureau of Land Management, Box 3388, Butte, MT 59702.

Marias River. BLM Fresno (#4) and Highwood (#14) maps show river downstream from the Highway 223 bridge almost to Loma. BLM 1:100,000 series map #38 shows most of the river above the Highway 223 bridge. Other maps hard to find.

Milk River. BLM Fresno (#4), Havre (#5), Belknap (#6), Bowdoin (#7), and Glasgow (#8) maps show entire river.

Missouri River. BLM Madison (#33) and Townsend (#23) maps cover entire Missouri below Canyon Ferry Reservoir; FS Helena National Forest map covers Missouri between Toston and Townsend. Montana DFW&P has a Missouri River Guide for the section from Holter Lake to Great Falls, available free by writing to Montana Department of Fish, Wildlife and Parks, Region 4 Headquarters, Route 4041, Great Falls, MT 59405. BLM 1:100,000 series map #40 covers from Craig to Great Falls; map #39 covers river from Great Falls to below Belt Creek.

The BLM has a special, two-part, waterproof floater's map for the wild and scenic section of the Missouri River. It offers details about the trip as well as a mile-by-mile report. It's available for $3 by writing to the Bureau of Land Management/Lewistown District, Airport Road, Lewistown, MT 59457. BLM maps Highwood (#14), Judith (#15), Breaks (#16), U.L. Bend (#17), Haxby (#18), Glasgow (#8), Poplar (#9), and Muddy (#10) cover the entire river from Fort Benton to the North Dakota border. Reprints of an 1891 river map (good detail of wild and scenic section plus historical sites) available from Glasgow Chamber of Commerce, Glasgow, MT 59230. Fair map of wild and scenic section plus good information available from Montana's DFW&P.

Red Rock River. BLM Red Rock (#41) and Centennial (#42) cover entire river; FS Beaverhead National Forest map covers entire river. U.S. Fish and Wildlife Service

(Red Rock Lakes National Wildlife Refuge, Monida Star Route, Lima, MT 59739) has a detailed map of the river between Upper Red Rock Lake and Lower Red Rock Lake.

Ruby River. BLM Dillon (#32) map covers entire river. FS Beaverhead National Forest map covers entire river.

Smith River. Montana DFW&P has excellent Smith River float map that covers from the Fort Logan Bridge to the Eden Bridge; it's available for free by writing to Montana DFW&P Region 4 Headquarters at Route 4041, Great Falls, MT 59405. FS Helena National Forest map covers the river upstream from Tenderfoot Creek; FS Lewis and Clark National Forest map (Jefferson Division) shows the river upstream from Eden Bridge; BLM Townsend map (#23) shows the river above Tenderfoot Creek; BLM 1:100,000 series map #39 shows river from Tenderfoot Creek to the Missouri.

Stillwater River. BLM Beartooth (#35) map covers entire river; FS Custer National Forest map (Beartooth Division-west half) covers entire river.

Sun River. BLM 1:100,000 series maps #29 and #29 show entire river; FS Lewis and Clark National Forest map (Rocky Mountain Division) shows river upstream from Highway 278 bridge.

Swan River. BLM 1:100,000 series maps #19 and #29 show entire river; FS Flathead National Forest maps (north or south half) show the river downstream from Salmon Prairie.

Tongue River. BLM Tongue (#38) and Custer (#29) maps cover entire river; FS Custer National Forest map (Ashland Division) covers the river above Brandenberg.

Yellowstone River. BLM Maps Park (#34), Beartooth (#35), Pryor (#36), Sumatra (#27), Rosebud (#28), Custer (#29), Fallon (#30), and Savage (#20), cover entire river; FS Gallatin National Forest map shows the river upstream from Livingston; FS Custer National Forest map (Beartooth Division) shows the river from Big Timber to Billings. Montana DFW&P has an outstanding map of the river from Billings to the Missouri confluence called "Treasure of Gold." The small book contains detailed maps, historical information, and biological details; it's highly recommended. It's available for $1 by writing to the Montana Department of Fish, Wildlife and Parks main office in Helena. It's also available at regional offices in Billings and Miles City.

Here are the addresses for the agencies which produce maps:

> Bureau of Land Management, Montana State Office
> 222 N. 32nd St., Box 30157
> Billings, MT 59107

> U.S. Forest Service
> Northern Region Headquarters, Federal Building
> Box 7669
> Missoula, MT 59807

> Montana Department of Fish, Wildlife and Parks
> 1420 East Sixth Avenue
> Helena, MT 59624

> U.S. Geological Survey
> Denver Distribution Section
> Federal Center, Building 41
> Denver, CO 80225

Appendix IV: Suggested reading

A Citizen's Guide to River Conservation. This is an excellent how-to book for people who are trying to develop river conservation programs. It offers case studies and innovative approaches from all over the country. It's available for $9.95 from the Conservation Foundation, 1255 23rd Street W., Washington, DC 20037.

Winning Strategies for Rivers. This outstanding publication is the proceedings from the 10th annual National Conference on Rivers. It's a series of papers on various river protection strategies, presented from a local, state, and national point of view. One of the papers involves creation of a cooperative river corridor program on Montana's Blackfoot River. The book is available for $10 from the American Rivers Conservation Council, 322 4th Street NE, Washington, DC 20002.

A Handbook on the Wild and Scenic Rivers Act. This handbook includes the text of the Wild and Scenic Rivers Act, a section-by-section review of the Act and compilation of the amendments to the Act. It's available by writing to the Wilderness Institute, University of Montana, Missoula, MT 59812. It sells for $1.50.

Flowing Free. This small paperback explains the basics of river protection. It discusses the National Wild and Scenic Rivers Act, state programs, and other alternatives for protection. In addition, this excellent book provides case studies (one is the Missouri River in Montana) of how three different rivers gained protection. It's available from the River Conservation Fund, 322 4th St., NE, Washington, DC 20036. It costs $4 per copy, and quantity prices are available upon request. This publication is a bit dated, but still useful.

Hank Fischer

Hank Fischer, 36, has been floating Montana rivers for many years and has written about them in publications like *Canoe, Backpacker, Sierra,* and *Montana Outdoors.* He received a master's degree from the University of Montana in Environmental Studies, and for the last 10 years has worked full-time for Defenders of Wildlife as their Northern Rockies field representative; he also does regular conservation commentary for Montana public radio. He lives in Missoula with his wife Carol and their two sons.

Publisher's note

In preparing *The Floater's Guide to Montana* for publication (it was originally published in 1979 and revised in 1983), the author and publisher went the extra mile to assure accuracy and completeness, thus necessitating yet another major revision in 1986. At the same time, however, we realize that any such work is inherently incomplete and outdated. Each year, nature changes the river channel, and access becomes more or less available.

In our previous publication, we invited floaters to write us, sending their suggestions and criticism, to help us patch any holes we may have missed in the previous printings. We are very grateful for the letters and advice we have received from our readers.

Because of your help, we believe this publication to be one of the most accurate, useful guides possible.

Falcon Press Publishing Co., Inc.
P.O. Box 731
Helena, MT 59601